C000175832

ALEXANDRA DUDLEY

# LAND & SEA

ALEXANDRA DUDLEY

# LAND & SEA

Secrets to simple, sustainable, sensational food

*For my Oma and Opa pa.*
*Thinking of you always.*

## Contents

# Introduction

They say food is medicine. For me, I think it's the cooking that is the medicine – the peeling, chopping, rolling and stirring, the waiting while the dough rises, and everything in between. It is in these simple acts that I find peace of mind, and if I ever feel wobbly with life, spending time in the kitchen brings me back to my roots.

My mother always made sure that the kitchen was the heart of the home. The space was sacred, with conscious care taken over every detail – from choosing the colour of the paint on the walls to deciding where the wooden spoons should be kept. The kitchen was where we spent most of our time, and I think that's true for most families. It's where you'll find the blotchy children's self-portraits pinned to the fridge, it's where the smell of Sunday lunch comes from, it's where we make the coffee and it's where (generally) the dog sleeps.

I have had a fascination with the kitchen since I was a child – from watching my mother and grandmother cook to learning to do things for myself. I can still remember, aged seven, going through about 16 eggs one early Mothering Sunday morning in an attempt to produce the perfect fried egg, while my sister eagerly waited by the toaster, ready for the call to action to push down the bread. My mother liked her toast piping hot with a generous amount of melted, slightly salted butter. Needless to say, I don't think either the egg or the toast were hot by the time it reached her but I think she enjoyed it all the same – and since then I have learned to cook an excellent fried egg!

I enjoyed school, but as a hopeless daydreamer I preferred my ballet classes or Wednesday afternoons in the art room. The things I could do were sing, paint and bake. Little drawings and occasional 'sofa-staged' performances were well received but nothing went down quite as well as edible goods. My Chocolate toffee crunch (see page 202), based on the much-loved Daim bar (a delicious combination of crunchy hazelnut-studded toffee coated in chocolate), is still today one of my signature Christmas gifts.

My inclination towards kitchen experiments drew me to investigating the methods of what I then called 'proper cooking'. I ripped out recipes from Sunday papers and spent my weekend afternoons losing myself in my mother's cookbooks. These were the Mary Berry and Delia Smith days (good, good days), but my favourite book of all was one on French patisserie, which had a giant illustration of a croissant on the front. I couldn't understand a word of it but I would spend hours tracing the intricate pastry diagrams. The kitchen was my home, it was where I could shine and it was where I could make other people smile.

I wrote my first recipe book when I was 11, and many of those Sunday afternoon pastry tracings featured proudly in the neat(ish) cartoon-strip directions to 'Alexandra's cookbook'. It had four recipes. There was an English apple tart, heavily influenced by its French sister but made with English apples from the garden and blackberry jam instead of apricot – after all, we were in England. Then came my chocolate toffee crunch, butterfly fairy cakes and peanut butter cookies.

Most of my childhood recipes were influenced by the cookbooks I loved at the time. Helen Drew's *My First Baking Book* still has the best peanut butter cookie recipe I know. However, my rebellious streak outed itself early in the kitchen; hence my recipes always had a twist. Determined to make them my own, I'd swap walnuts for hazelnuts, double the honey and leave out the salt, or use basil instead of mint. The aim was always to wow and create something unusual – although fondly remembered failures include the lavender ice cream that made my mouth taste like soap for days, gooseberry custard which looked more like witches' potion and countless batches of failed scones.

Thankfully I made my peace with each of these failed recipes and found my way with them, and even the ugly disasters make me smile. The failing didn't matter; it was just an excuse to try again. Over the years that itch to experiment continues to grow; the curiosity for new and varied ingredients is ever increasing, especially when I travel, and I hope I will always seek new recipes to adapt and adopt in my own little kitchen.

I think the best people are those that suffer from wanderlust. For me, the syndrome is left over from hearing stories of my mother's childhood in Africa, my grandfather sneaking back coconuts in his suitcase, and afternoons watching Disney films with my siblings. Daydreaming also had a lot to do with it. When my German grandmother, or Oma, visited she would tell us the greatest bedtime stories; our favourite was the 'magic carpet'. Oma would let us choose where we wanted to go and we'd all say, India! The story would then be about two little girls and one boy, a magic carpet and their journey through Mumbai. The funny thing is, my grandmother never went to India or any of the places we went to on the carpet, but these games fuelled my desire to see them in reality.

Although India is still on my list, since then I've been lucky enough to visit many of the places we went to on the carpet. On every trip my main interest has been in the food – the native produce, traditions, tips and tricks from the locals. I like to make friends wherever I go and, never having been afraid to talk to strangers, have met some of the most wonderful and inspiring people along the way. Always, we have connected over a love of food and, for the most part, a love of nature. Food and nature go hand in hand. The best food comes straight from the ground, tree and water, not from a can or packaging. The best meals are those made from these real ingredients, cooked fresh and that very often – at least in my case – have a little story behind them.

# A sustainable rhythm of eating

I suppose the rhythm of my eating has been heavily influenced by my upbringing. I was lucky enough to be brought up on home-cooked food, and with a strong European heritage, the table was often scattered with various plates of fresh salads, cold cuts and leftovers. Still today I have a firm rule to never throw anything away. There is always something to be rehashed from leftovers and more often than not I will cook with those in mind. The cook once eat twice mentality is incredibly useful, especially when you live a busy, fast-paced life, which so many of us do.

During the week breakfasts are quick and easy – yoghurt, fruit and oats are all regular contenders. Hot water and lemon followed by strong hot coffee or tea is compulsory, as is BBC Radio 4. Lunch is usually a mix of leftovers dressed up with something fresh and colourful. I am a regular packed-lunch eater and have been making them since I was an art student, partly because it saved money, but primarily because I found, and still find, that generally I enjoy them more than a soggy sandwich or barren salad.

Dinner is where things get a little more exciting, but as a general rule it will be something that takes under an hour to pull together. Despite weekday meals being a little less fancy than those that I prepare at the weekend, there is no compromise on flavour. Thursday night's dinner may be Rosemary bream with roasted romanesco, lemon and battered olives (page 116) alongside a zingy Avocado and yellow pepper smash (page 180). Or maybe Warm roasted courgette, cavalo nero and sunflower seed salad (page 90) topped with a soft poached egg, a dip of some sort (pages 238–240) and some crusty sourdough. It may sound extravagant, but the truth is most of what we eat during the week is cooked and on the table in under 40 minutes.

It's a common misconception that delicious food must be fancy or fussy, or that it requires spending hours in the kitchen, and these recipes are testament that this is not the case. All one needs is a little planning, and by that I do not mean piling identically filled containers ready for the week ahead. More of a poke in the fridge in the morning, noticing that you have some courgettes on their way out and thinking, 'I might just grab a few leeks and tomatoes and make my Shepherdless pie' (page 152).

True, a well-stocked pantry cupboard makes things easier, but again I am not talking an A–Z of spices. There are a few staples (see pages 12–15) that I return to time and time again. Generally, they carry bold flavour as well as the benefit of a long shelf life, meaning you need to use very little and purchase them only on occasion.

For me, cooking dinner is my down time. It's the way I unwind after a stressful day, switch off from work and spend quality time with my friends, family and boyfriend. I try to implement a 'no phones after 8pm' rule and certainly not at the table. That way there is more room for laughter, chatter and truly enjoying the food.

On the weekend our eating patterns are slower, more cosy. There is a little more flexibility with meal times, so often this is when I have space to experiment. My Hake, prawn and lemongrass curry soup (page 46) is great for early on a Sunday evening if we've eaten a late heavy breakfast and a couple more than a couple of slices of cake.

I love to go out to try new things, too, so as a treat we will visit one of London's new pop-ups or revisit much-loved restaurants, but weekends in the kitchen are still my favourite. I am never more excited than when we are throwing a dinner party and I'll note down at least fifteen different menus before I eventually settle on what to cook, only to then be distracted by some delicious-looking ingredient at the market and add just another thing, 'you know, in case people get hungry later on'. If you are ever hungry, come to my house, for there are usually at least four or five different offerings!

I am very much a seasonal eater and as I have grown older I have become even more so. What we choose to eat has both an effect on our taste buds and our health, as well as on our planet. Sustainability and being eco-friendly have become a real topic in recent years, with solar panels and wind turbines increasingly becoming the norm, and as a part of that eating sustainably is gaining popularity. It is something that I believe deserves conscious effort. Whilst I am neither vegan nor vegetarian (nor paleo, pescatarian or whatever else one can be dubbed as today), I do believe in thinking carefully when choosing my food, to consider the impact of my choice. I think the answer is not to eliminate all meat and dairy or to never touch tuna or avocados, but rather to eat consciously and with the world in mind. A whole, cooked, free-range organic chicken will go a lot further than budget chicken breasts. You could roast it with rosemary and lemon, enjoy leftovers thrown into salad and finish by making a warm and hearty soup from its broth. The taste is far better, as is the ecological effect.

I am a big believer in working with what you have. If I haven't been able to get to the butcher or fishmonger, we will eat vegetarian or go for a few organic, free-range eggs for a dose of protein. Most of the recipes in here are designed to be interchanged and played with, depending on what you have to hand. You could choose to make Pan-fried miso sea bass fillets (page 98) but enjoy it with a Sweet carrot and hazelnut salad (page 88) or perhaps three or four sides (pages 159–181). My intention is that the recipes are seen as guidelines rather than rigid instructions. My hope is that they also inspire you to be creative and perhaps a little daring in the kitchen.

What fascinates me most about cooking is how the opportunities for new things are simply endless. There is never a point that one reaches where one knows it all; there is always more to learn, more to play with. In a sense, the kitchen and cooking keeps us young and on our toes. I've always had a slight Peter Pan mentality, and while I used to think of it as something I needed to grow out of, I now embrace it. My grandmother once told me that we never stop growing; somewhere either in mind or heart there is something to be learned or discovered, some plant to water and watch grow. I couldn't agree more.

# Cupboard staples

**There are a few ingredients that I seem to return to time and time again, and which very often make all the difference when trying to create the perfect meal. While some are a little more exotic, in general all the ingredients listed here are easy to find. If you cannot find them in your local supermarket, the nearest health food store should have them in stock.**

## Good-quality olive oil

I go for cold-pressed olive oil for use in dressings. The taste is so much richer and you get that wonderful peppery zing. Keep it for use raw, don't waste the good stuff in frying. For cooking go for a good-quality extra-virgin. Italian or Greek is best and most supermarkets have a good selection.

## Coconut oil

A brilliant oil for high-heat cooking as it can withstand the heat. It has a mild coconut flavour which I do enjoy, especially when cooking Asian-inspired dishes. Go for butter or rapeseed oil if you don't like the coconutty taste.

## Cold-pressed rapeseed oil

Golden in colour and with a gentle taste and a high-heat stability, rapeseed oil is wonderful for roasting vegetables or frying fish or meat. If a recipe calls for butter and you are trying to avoid dairy but are not a fan of the flavour of coconut oil, this is a great substitute – not least because it can simply be drizzled over rather than waiting for coconut oil to melt.

## Grass-fed organic butter

There are few things that don't taste better with butter. As with all animal products, my advice is to go for the best quality – and that means grass-fed and organic. For baking and most cooking I would go unsalted, but a little slightly salted butter spread over some hot toast is one of life's simple pleasures. I get my butter at my local weekend market. It keeps for a while, too, so I am rarely out of it. If you are following a vegan diet, coconut oil works well in the place of butter and in all my recipes I give suggestions for vegan alternatives.

## Toasted sesame oil

Incredibly potent, this oil is made from the toasted hull of the sesame seed. I love the smell of toasted sesame oil and always take a long sniff whenever I open up a bottle. Use it with care as the taste can be strong. I generally use it to make nutty dressings which I drizzle over cooked food but it can have its uses in marinades, too (Quick miso 'black' halibut with candied leeks page 108).

## Miso paste

A traditional Japanese seasoning, miso paste is a rich, slightly sweet, slightly salty paste made from fermented soya beans and often rice or barley. Delicious in sauces and dressings, it also makes a wonderful marinade for meat or fish. I usually go for brown rice miso paste as I love the depth of flavour. White rice miso paste is slightly sweeter but is delicious as a more subtle marinade or an accompaniment to potatoes, cauliflower or other starchy vegetables.

## Tamari

To me, tamari is quite the magic ingredient. Similar to miso in that it is made from fermenting soya beans, it has a wickedly deep taste which is described as umami. Although often purely considered to be a gluten-free relative of soya sauce, the taste of tamari is richer and a little less salty. There can at times be a very small amount of wheat or gluten present in the making of tamari but in most cases the fermenting process diminishes the gluten content. I would mention that for anyone who is following a specifically gluten-free diet or suffers from coeliac disease it is worth making sure you go for a top-quality tamari or one that is certified gluten free. Tamari is delicious in dressings and soups, useful when roasting vegetables and/or fish and meat, and can take many things from bland to brilliant.

## Dijon mustard

I must go through at least a jar of this every two weeks. My failsafe salad dressing, which also works on roasted or steamed vegetables, is two parts cold-pressed olive oil to one part apple cider vinegar and a spoonful (size depending) of Dijon mustard. I love to watch a gloopy, almost hollandaise-like dressing form in the bottom of a wooden salad bowl whilst I whisk away with a little fork. Dijon mustard is delicious in marinades, too, or even stirred into sauces or mashes (see Shepherdless pie page 152).

## Good salt

It may seem insignificant but a tiny pinch of salt can take a meal from bland to bouncing off your taste buds. I love coarse sea salt flakes but it can be useful to have some good-quality fine sea salt in the house, too, especially for baking.

## Spices

I am a keen user of spices and my travels to Morocco and Greece always result in bags upon bags of glorious colourful spices coming home with me. If you ever get the opportunity to visit Morocco, be prepared to want to bring back half the souk. You'll find that the majority of these spices are in fact available in most supermarkets nowadays but I often stumble across some incredibly exotic ones at Middle Eastern specialist shops or food markets. Spice preference is down to personal taste, so my advice would be to collect what you like and be creative with your seasoning. Although often reserved for cooking, spices can also make delicious additions to dressings, too. A pinch of cumin can take a simple olive oil and lemon dressing to another level.

Listed below are the spices that I use most often in this book, but if you cannot find some of them, do not panic. You can always try substituting for another spice to ring the changes.

*Ground cinnamon*
*Ground ginger*
*Ground turmeric*
*Ground mixed spice*
*Ground cumin*
*Ground coriander*
*Whole coriander seed*
*Cardamom pods*
*Ground cloves*
*Ground or whole nutmeg*
*Harissa spice*
*Z'atar*
*Sumac*
*Smoked paprika*
*Dried oregano*

## Herbs

Fresh herbs are my not-so-secret ingredient for everything and I probably use them in every meal I cook – even breakfast. (Basil and mint are, in fact, wonderful additions to fresh fruit and yoghurt, or even sprinkled over eggs.) If you can, invest in a few pot plants or grow them in a windowbox. Rosemary and thyme, in particular, are quite resilient in the British climate and need little pampering, but it's sensible to keep basil and coriander on a windowsill indoors as they are a little more delicate. When picking basil always pick the leaves from the bottom of the stem, choosing those with longer stems first as it is a sign that they are ready. Be sure to pick from the bottom of the plant, too. Make sure the soil is damp but that the roots are not drowning – basil is quite a thirsty plant so it's a good idea to check it daily if you can. With a little attention, your plant can last for months and you'll get a lot more basil for your money and always have fresh herbs to hand.

## Toasted nuts and seeds

I am a bit of a nut and seed fanatic; almonds, cashews, pistachios, sunflower seeds – I have a soft spot for them all. I adore the nutty crunch that they add to recipes and always have a few jam jars filled with one or the other so that they are there at the ready when something needs a bit more bite. For suggestions on different ways to toast nuts and seeds, see pages 244–5.

### Pomegranate molasses

Undoubtedly more of an exotic ingredient, pomegranate molasses is a thick, dark syrupy liquid that is popular in Middle Eastern cooking. It adds an indulgent richness to meat, fish or vegetable dishes and makes a wonderful dressing. You can find it in most supermarkets now and all health stores.

### A word on flour

I use spelt flour in most recipes because I adore its nutty taste. However, because it has a low gluten content it is also incredibly popular with most gluten-sensitive tummies. The difference between wholegrain and white spelt flour is significant, too. The white variety is closer to plain white flour and the wholegrain is a little richer and stronger in taste. Where I haven't specified, either works well. If you don't like spelt flour or can't get your hands on it you can always use regular plain flour (ideally wholegrain rather than white for its nutritional value). If you're gluten-intolerant, go for alternative flours like buckwheat or rice. I tend to mix a little of each to get more of a rounded flavour.

## Equipment

**Most cooking can be done with a decent knife, a chopping board and a few pans, bowls and spoons – but there are a few kitchen items that have definitely made my life easier . . .**

### Stick blender

Brilliant for preparing salsas, dips, mashes and soups and avoiding the faff of having to transfer hot vegetables to a blender. My poor blender hardly gets a look-in nowadays. The great thing about these is the ease with which they can be washed up as well as the fact that they store very neatly, taking up little space. A real bonus in a compact kitchen like my little one.

### Garlic crusher

For those of you who want to avoid the dreaded garlic fingers, this is a must. A word of advice is to go for a good-quality, heavyweight one. Mine is made by Oxo and I have had it for over a decade. You may spend a few extra pounds getting a good one, but it is worth it.

### Food processor

Useful for many things such as making pastry, blending dips, grinding nuts into nut butter or finely chopping herbs. If space is limited in your kitchen you can get relatively compact versions nowadays. Although not an essential piece of kit, a good food processor does come in handy.

# Rules of Thumb

## Use the whole ingredient

I see it all the time, people chopping off perfectly edible bits of courgette or carrots and tossing them into the bin. Whenever I ask why they reply, 'oh, but you can't eat that bit' but this is simply a myth. When eating courgettes, one can eat the whole thing; there is no need to cut away any of it. The stem part is utterly delicious roasted and is often the part we fight over in my house. It's the same for carrots – the end bits may look a little gnarly but they taste perfectly fine. You may just want to brush off any dirt.

The stalks and stems of broccoli and cauliflower and the tougher stems of kale or even herbs can all be put to good use, too. They may just require a little longer cooking, finer chopping or perhaps are destined to be turned into comforting soups. These bits are truly just as delicious as their perfectly groomed counterparts. (See Basil broccoli stalk mash, page 166.) And any bits that you really don't want to eat will make a delicious stock.

## Make stock

People often ask about the strange bowl of onion skin and vegetable offcuts that sits in my fridge, asking if I 'have a miniature compost heap stashed away on my balcony or something'. The question always makes me giggle because honestly I wish I did but my window terrace is a touch small and I am not sure if my neighbours would approve.

The bowl is in fact my 'stock bowl'. At least once a week I will make stock from these collected offcuts. Sometimes it is purely a vegetable stock, sometimes it will be a chicken stock, using the carcass from a roast. The finished stock will either be kept in the fridge to be added to soups or warmed through and sipped on as a comforting broth, or frozen in small portions so that it's on hand when I need it.

There are, of course, times when I forget to make use of the stock bowl and the peelings go rancid. I am not perfect and, as is frequently the case in life, time often slips away. But the intention is there, and of all the habits I have this is certainly a good one.

Making stock really couldn't be simpler; all it requires is a decent amount of vegetable scraps or bones and enough water to cover them, which can then be left on a low simmer for a couple of hours. Another trick is to add to your stock. If I am cooking a big dinner on Friday night and know that we have people over for Sunday lunch, I will do the first simmer on Saturday morning then leave it to cool and add to it on Sunday. Doing this adds depth to your stock and a few ladlefuls spooned into a small saucepan to boil up a few peas and wilt some spinach, perhaps with a little shredded chicken, makes for a wonderful Sunday night supper.

## Be creative with your herbs and spices

The recipes in this book are intended to be used as guidelines only, not a strict set of instructions. If the recipe calls for coriander and you only have basil, use the basil. If I have said a teaspoon of ground cumin and you either hate it or only have ground coriander, go for it. Each of our tastes are different and cooking is so much about instinct, so go with your gut. Often I find my most successful recipes come about from either accidents or emergency substitutions. That is where the magic of cooking really starts.

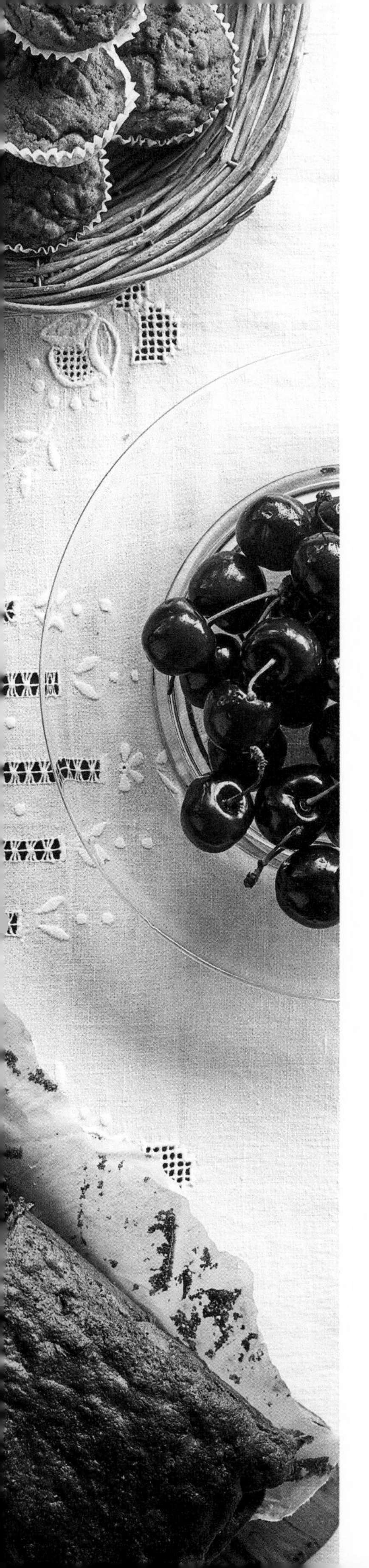

# Mornings

Mornings are sacred in my house. As a child I would wake up at the crack of dawn to wave my father off as he cycled to work before climbing back into bed, tummy rumbling, to eagerly wait for my mother's call that it was breakfast time. Breakfast was, and still is, the most important meal of the day for me, and no matter what happens I never miss it.

During the working week I usually eat something that is quick to prepare, such as oats soaked overnight, scrambled eggs or a slice of my Spelt, honey and walnut loaf (see page 20) with some crunchy peanut butter. I like simple and not overly sweet food in the morning. Texture is also important to me, so whatever I am eating will usually be topped with some toasted nuts, seeds, coconut, or whatever I can find in the row of jars that line my counter top.

It is the weekend, though, when I most enjoy breakfast. I love cooking for others and there is no greater satisfaction for me than when my family and friends bumble down the stairs on Sunday morning to be met with a table laden with hot coffee, fresh fruit and something I have baked that very morning.

This loaf is similar to the dense German rye bread or Roggenbrot that my grandmother used to make, but in this version I use spelt flour for its nutty taste. Although the bread contains honey it really isn't very sweet and can be enjoyed both with cheese and cold meats (very continental) or toasted with butter and jam. I like mine with a good spread of crunchy peanut butter. The key to baking bread, as my grandmother always said, is patience, so take your time making the dough and do not skimp on rising time or you'll be left with a very tough loaf. Even though these loaves don't have a huge amount of height to them, the proving is still important.

## Spelt, honey and walnut loaf

**Makes 2 medium-sized loaves**

*500g spelt flour, plus extra for dusting*

*7g dried active baking yeast (do not use fast-action)*

*1 tbsp clear honey*

*350ml tepid water*

*1 tsp salt*

*70g walnuts, chopped*

*rapeseed oil, for greasing*

*1 egg yolk, lightly beaten*

Place 50g of the flour, the yeast, honey and 50ml of the water in a small bowl. Mix well, cover with a dry cloth and leave in a warm place for about 30 minutes or until the mixture has started to bubble slightly.

In a very large bowl, combine the rest of the flour, the salt and walnuts and add the yeast mixture with the rest of the water. Stir to combine and tip your dough onto a clean, lightly oiled work surface. The dough will be sticky – this is normal.

Roughly shape the dough into a ball and, using the heel of your hand, push the dough away from you as though you are stretching it, before pulling it back again. Give the dough a quarter of a turn and repeat this process for 10–15 minutes.

Your dough is ready when it passes the window test. Cut off a small piece of the dough and stretch it between your fingers, holding it up to the light. If you can stretch it thin enough to see light shining through without it breaking it, it is ready, Don't be afraid to be quite tough on the dough.

Clean and dry the bowl then lightly grease it with a little oil. Lightly flour the kneaded dough and place it in the bowl. Cover with a clean dry tea towel or cling film and leave it to rise in a warm place for about an hour or until doubled in size. Depending on the temperature this may take more or less time, but do make sure your dough has fully swelled.

Line two baking sheets with baking parchment and dust these with flour. Once the dough is ready, turn it out onto a floured surface and, using a large knife, slice it in half, reshaping each half into a ball.

Place each ball on a baking sheet and gently cover with a clean dry tea towel or cling film, put in a warm place and allow the loaves to rise again for 20 minutes.

Preheat the oven to 200°C/400°F/gas mark 6.

Using a pastry brush, gently paint the beaten egg yolk over the loaves and, using a sharp knife, make a slight slit down the centre of each. You could also make criss-cross patterns. Place the loaves in the oven and bake for about 40 minutes or until risen and nicely browned. To check they are cooked, tap the base of one and see if it sounds hollow. If you are not getting a good sound back, they may need a little longer.

Remove from the oven and turn out the loaves onto a wire rack, dust with a little extra flour and leave them to cool completely.

There is something blissfully naughty about French toast – sticky and sweet and usually doused in maple syrup, it feels as though one is having pudding for breakfast. This recipe uses banana bread as the base, so the finished dish feels even more decadent. I always have a bag or two of berries stored in the freezer, kept from summer and autumn. You can, of course, use fresh berries in season, but oddly enough I prefer frozen as they release their juices quickly when warmed on the hob. The banana bread itself is quite delicious 'un-Frenched', too, and makes for a lovely afternoon tea, especially when slathered in some of my homemade Espresso butter (page 236).

# Banana bread French toast

*with warm-off-the-hob blueberries*

**Makes 1 loaf and serves 2 as French toast**

***For the banana loaf***

*110g coconut oil or butter, melted, plus extra for greasing*

*50g walnuts*

*230g flour (I like wholemeal spelt but plain or a gluten-free blend work too)*

*80g light brown soft sugar or coconut sugar*

*1 tsp ground cinnamon*

*½ tsp ground nutmeg*

*1 tsp baking powder*

*¼ tsp bicarbonate of soda*

*pinch of salt*

*5 ripe bananas, mashed*

*2 large eggs, lightly beaten*

*1 tsp vanilla extract*

Begin by making the banana loaf. It helps to have made this at least the evening before. Preheat the oven to 180°C/350°F/gas mark 4 and grease a 20 x 10cm loaf pan and line with baking parchment.

Place the walnuts on a dry baking tray and toast in the oven for about 8 minutes or until fragrant. Allow them to cool before roughly chopping.

In a large bowl, whisk together the flour, sugar, cinnamon, nutmeg, baking powder, bicarbonate of soda and salt. Stir in the chopped walnuts.

In a medium-sized bowl, combine the bananas, eggs, melted coconut oil or butter and vanilla.

Lightly fold the wet ingredients into the dry until just combined – the mixture should still contain a few lumps. Pour the batter into the prepared loaf tin and bake for about 50 minutes or until a wooden skewer inserted into the centre of the loaf comes out mostly clean with no more than a few crumbs.

Transfer the tin to a wire rack and allow the cake to cool completely in the tin. If you are out of eggs or don't fancy French toast, the banana bread is delicious as it is, or try it with a lashing of my Espresso butter over it (page 236). If you want to make the banana bread into French toast, slice the loaf into no thinner than 1.5cm pieces – too thin and they will break.

In a medium-sized bowl, whisk the eggs and sugar together to combine. Put your frying pan over a medium heat, add a knob of butter or coconut oil and melt.

*For the 'Frenching'*

*2 eggs*

*1 tbsp coconut or light brown soft sugar*

*Coconut oil or butter, for frying*

*For the blueberries*

*100g blueberries (frozen work best)*

*2 tsp coconut sugar or honey (optional)*

*maple syrup, to serve (optional)*

In a separate saucepan, gently warm the berries. For the sweeter inclined, add some sugar and stir every so often.

One by one, dip the loaf slices into the egg mix, turning them once or twice in it before transferring to the hot pan. While the first side is cooking you may want to drop roughly a teaspoon more of the egg mix on top as some may naturally slide down the side of the toast as it cooks. After about 2 minutes, gently flip the toast and cook for the same amount of time on the other side or until golden.

Serve the hot toast with a generous tablespoon of the warmed blueberries and some maple syrup, if you fancy some extra sweetness.

It is an annual tradition that every summer my father and I walk out to Scolt Head Island, an offshore sandy haven about an hour's walk from my family home in Brancaster Staithe. On the day of the walk I wake early in the morning to make a batch of these muffins and wrap half a dozen of them in a tea towel straight from the oven. They are still warm by the time we arrive at the island and together we will sit on the sand and share coffee from a flask while making our way through the muffins and sharing village gossip. Packed full of nuts, seeds, fruit and vegetables, we often joke that these muffins contain nearly everything that lines the pantry shelves, so they're now fondly referred to as 'everything muffins'.

# Everything muffins

**Makes 12**

*2 large carrots, peeled and grated*

*1 apple, peeled and grated*

*175g spelt flour*

*100g light brown soft sugar or coconut sugar*

*½ tsp baking powder*

*1 tsp bicarbonate of soda*

*pinch of salt*

*1 tsp ground cinnamon*

*½ tsp mixed spice*

*50g pecans or walnuts, toasted (see page 245) and chopped*

*20g rolled oats*

*20g pumpkin seeds*

*1 tbsp poppy or chia seeds*

*2 large eggs*

*120ml rapeseed oil or butter or coconut oil, melted*

*1 tsp vanilla extract*

*1 ripe banana, mashed*

Line a 12-holed muffin tray with squares of baking parchment or paper cases and preheat the oven to 180°C/350°F/gas mark 4.

Combine the grated carrots and apple and set aside.

In a large bowl, whisk together the flour, sugar, baking powder, bicarbonate of soda, salt, cinnamon and mixed spice. Stir in the chopped nuts, oats, pumpkin and chia or poppy seeds.

In a separate bowl, whisk together the eggs, oil or butter and vanilla. Stir in the mashed banana until combined.

Pour the banana-egg mix, grated carrots and apple into the flour and fold gently to combine, stirring just until incorporated – a few lumps are fine. The trick to muffins is to not over-stir the batter – as soon as the mix is incorporated, they are ready to go.

Divide the batter between the paper cases and bake for 20–25 minutes or until a wooden skewer inserted into the centre comes out mostly clean with no more than a few crumbs.

Allow the muffins to cool in the tin for about 10 minutes, then remove them and allow them to cool completely on a wire rack, or eat them while still warm.

These pancakes are a staple of my weekend breakfast feasts. What I love most about them is that they work for both the savoury lovers and the sweet-toothed. If, like me, you have more of a savoury palate in the mornings, you can enjoy them just as they are or with a knob of slightly salted butter or chopped avocado. If you prefer a sweeter breakfast, there is the option to add blueberries or an extra tablespoon of coconut sugar, or – even better – drench the cooked pancakes in sticky maple syrup or honey.

## Basic breakfast oat pancakes

**Makes 8–10**

*30g rolled oats*

*120g white spelt or plain white flour (a good gluten-free blend will work too)*

*2 tbsp light brown soft sugar or coconut sugar*

*1 tbsp baking powder*

*½ tsp salt*

*150ml organic, whole milk (or oat or almond)*

*1 large egg*

*25g unsalted butter, melted and slightly cooled*

*butter or coconut oil, for frying*

*80g blueberries (optional)*

Begin by toasting your oats in a dry pan over a medium heat for about 5 minutes or until they begin to smell nutty. Transfer to a plate and allow them to cool fully.

In a large bowl, sift together your flour, sugar, baking powder and salt.

In a separate smaller bowl, beat together your milk and egg until fully incorporated. Add in your butter and whisk well.

Pour wet ingredients into dry and whisk until just incorporated, adding your oats halfway through. Be sure not to over-mix or you will get tough pancakes; a few lumps are fine.

In a large frying pan, melt a knob of butter or coconut oil over a medium heat before cooking the pancakes in batches of 2, using about 2 tablespoons of the mix for each.

Cook for roughly 3–4 minutes or until you see bubbles forming. Then flip your pancake, cooking the other side for a further 2–3 minutes.

If you are adding blueberries do this as soon as you see the bubbles start to form.

Serve warm with your toppings of choice.

I love the story behind the Cornish pasty – it gained its characteristic D shape way back in the nineteenth century when it was a bite to eat for the Cornish miners. Its crust was originally used as a disposable handle, allowing the miners to hold and eat the pie without it getting grubby. Pasties are traditionally filled with meat and potato so I suspect this fruity version would have been a little too dainty for the miners. It does, however, make a wonderfully sweet breakfast with some yoghurt, and can double up as a summer pudding, too, with cream or ice cream.

# Little nectarine and berry pasties

**Makes about 14–16 small pasties**

*1 nectarine (about 125g when chopped)*

*150g strawberries*

*1 tbsp lemon juice*

*½ tsp vanilla powder*

*2 tbsp light brown soft sugar or coconut sugar (optional), plus extra for sprinkling*

***For the pastry***

*250g white spelt or plain flour, plus extra for dusting*

*pinch of salt*

*2 tbsp light brown soft sugar or coconut sugar, plus extra for sprinkling*

*100g butter, cold and chopped into pieces, or coconut oil*

*75–100ml ice-cold water, as needed*

*milk, for glazing*

***Equipment***

*Large round biscuit cutter (mine is 10cm)*

First make the pastry. In a large bowl or in the bowl of your food processor, combine the flour, salt and sugar. Using your fingers, rub the cold butter or coconut oil into the flour until the mixture resembles breadcrumbs. If you are using a food processor, give it a few pulses to do this. Slowly add the cold water and use your hands to combine or keep pulsing your processor until your dough comes together. Turn it out onto a lightly floured surface and shape it into a flat disc. Wrap in cling film and place in the fridge for roughly half an hour or until it has stiffened slightly.

When you are ready to bake, preheat the oven to 200°C/400°F/gas mark 6 and line a baking sheet with baking parchment.

Chop the nectarine and strawberries very small and combine in a bowl with the lemon juice and vanilla. Add the sugar, if you like.

Lightly flour a surface and roll out the chilled pastry to roughly ½cm thickness. Using a large round biscuit cutter, cut out pastry rounds. Reroll any pastry scraps to use as much of the pastry as you can.

Space the circles evenly on the baking tray and place a spoonful of the fruit mix into the middle of each one, leaving about a 3cm border. Fold over the pastry circles and pinch them shut around the edge using a fork. Brush the pastry with a little milk and sprinkle with a touch of sugar. Bake for 20 minutes or until the pastry is golden brown and the juice is slightly seeping out of the edges.

Allow them to cool slightly on the tray before gently removing with a spatula.

Despite the name, this recipe is borrowed from the German side of my family and not the Dutch. It was my German grandmother who taught me how to make these, using the same recipe that her mother taught her. This pancake is best served warm and eaten straight from the oven. Take care when removing it as the frying pan handle will be very hot. I find it needs little more than a pinch of cinnamon to serve, but you may like to drizzle over some honey or maple syrup if you have a sweeter tooth.

## Dutch baby *(apple-stuffed puffed pancake)*

**Serves 4**

*3 large eggs, at room temperature*

*75ml full-fat milk, or coconut milk, at room temperature*

*75g spelt flour (plain, buckwheat or gluten-free blend works too)*

*1 tsp vanilla extract*

*pinch of salt*

*1 tsp ground cinnamon, plus extra to dust (optional)*

*4 tbsp butter or coconut oil*

*1 large Pink Lady or Braeburn apple, peeled and sliced into ½cm slices*

*1–2 tbsp light brown soft sugar or coconut sugar*

*maple syrup or honey, to serve (optional)*

Preheat the oven to 200°C/400°F/gas mark 6.

In a medium-sized bowl, whisk the eggs, milk, flour, vanilla, salt and ½ teaspoon of the cinnamon to a smooth batter.

Melt 2 tablespoons of the butter or coconut oil in a medium-sized ovenproof frying pan over a medium heat. Add the apple, remaining cinnamon and the sugar. Cook until the apple has softened, gently turning the slices continuously so that they are evenly coated in the cinnamon sugar mix. Transfer to a plate and set aside before wiping your pan clean with some kitchen paper.

Place the pan in the oven for about 10 minutes then remove and melt the remaining 2 tablespoons of butter or oil in the pan. Tilt the pan to evenly coat the base and sides.

Return the apple to the pan and pour over the batter. Place the pan in the hot oven and bake for about 15 minutes or until the pancake has puffed up. The centre should still have a slight wobble and the outside be a nice golden-brown colour.

Make sure you are still wearing oven gloves, then cut the pancake directly in the pan and serve as you would a pie, sprinkling it with extra cinnamon, maple syrup or honey, if you wish.

A brilliant breakfast to fuel a big day, I love to make this before we head out for a country walk or a day outside. Kedgeree is warm and hearty and makes for delicious leftovers. I like to serve this right out of the pan, simply placed on the table so that everyone can dig in.

# Smoked haddock, cardamom and saffron kedgeree

**Serves 4–6**

*3 large parsnips, grated*

*4 tbsp coconut oil, rapeseed oil or butter*

*500g undyed smoked haddock, pin-boned and cut into 2–3 pieces*

*2 bay leaves*

*200g wholegrain or brown basmati rice*

*4 eggs*

*1 garlic clove, crushed*

*bunch of spring onions, finely chopped*

*pinch of saffron*

*6–8 cardamom pods*

*good pinch of sea salt*

*juice of 1 lemon*

*bunch of coriander, leaves roughly chopped, to serve*

*1 fresh red chilli, finely sliced, to serve (optional)*

First make your spice mix. Toast the coriander and cumin seeds in a dry frying pan over a medium heat until they begin to almost pop. Add the ginger, cinnamon, turmeric and cardamom seeds and stir over the heat for just a minute – you don't want to burn the spices. Remove from the heat and put the toasted spices, clove and peppercorns in a pestle and mortar or coffee bean/spice grinder and grind to a powder. Set aside. If you don't have a pestle and mortar I find that simply placing the spices in a small but sturdy bowl and using the spice jar itself to gently bash them down works well.

In a large pan, fry the parsnips in half the oil or butter for about 10 minutes over a medium heat or until they are cooked through and have become a little crispy on the outside. Transfer them to a plate and set aside.

Place the haddock into the same frying pan, skin side up. Add the bay leaves and pour over 500ml of water. Bring the water to a gentle simmer and cook for about 8 minutes or until the fish flakes easily. Gently remove the fish using a spatula and set aside.

Pour the fishy water into a saucepan and add the rice, making sure it is covered by the water. You may need to add a touch more water. Bring the water to the boil before covering the pan with a lid and simmering for 10 minutes. Check the pan occasionally to make sure the water has not all evaporated. You may need to add a little more water every so often. Turn off the heat and keep the lid on the pan for a further 5–8 minutes to allow the rice to absorb all the water.

*For the spice mix*

*2 tsp coriander seeds*

*1 tsp cumin seeds*

*1 tsp ground ginger*

*½ tsp ground cinnamon*

*½ tsp ground turmeric*

*2 tsp ground cardamom seeds*

*1 whole clove*

*1 tsp whole black peppercorns*

While the rice is cooking, boil the eggs in a separate pan of boiling water for 10 minutes before running them under cold water for a few minutes and peeling.

In the large pan, melt the remaining coconut oil or butter over a low heat. Add the spice mix, garlic and cooked rice and stir through the parsnips and chopped spring onions. Add the saffron, cardamom and salt and cook gently for about 5 minutes.

Flake over the cooked fish and squeeze over the lemon juice, then gently fold everything together. Quarter the eggs and cover the pan with a lid. Turn off the heat but leave the lid on for about 5 minutes.

Serve sprinkled with some fresh coriander leaves and some sliced chilli, if you like. Any leftovers can be eaten cold or transferred into an ovenproof dish and reheated slowly at 150°C/300°F/gas mark 2 for 25–30 minutes or until they are heated right through. Make sure that the centre of the dish is absolutely piping hot before eating.

I first made this rather cosy breakfast Boxing Day morning after finding a few lonely-looking carrots and parsnips in the larder that didn't make it to Christmas lunch. I teamed them with festive spices and a half-empty packet of sultanas (no doubt left over from baking the Christmas cake) – it went down a treat and was the perfect start to a day of festivities. You don't have to add the whiskey, but if you do you're guaranteed to put a smile on everyone's faces, not to mention some colour in their cheeks. Having made this many times now, I recommend leaving the ingredients to soak overnight, which allows the oats and sultanas to soften as well as making the porridge easier on the digestion.

# Rooty oats with whiskey-soaked sultanas

**Serves 4**

***For the porridge***

*200g jumbo oats*

*2 medium-sized carrots*

*2 small parsnips (small parsnips are sweeter)*

*zest of 1 orange*

*½ tsp ground cloves*

*1 tsp mixed spice*

*1½ tsp ground cinnamon*

*600ml milk of your choice (but I'd advise against coconut milk here)*

*roughly 70g sultanas*

*2 tbsp wild honey or maple syrup*

*3 tbsp whiskey*

***For the topping***

*70g sultanas*

*6 tbsp whiskey*

*2 tbsp boiling water from the kettle*

*60g raw pecans, chopped*

Wash, peel and grate your carrots and parsnips before placing them in a medium-size bowl along with the rest of the porridge ingredients. Stir to combine and leave in a cool larder or fridge overnight. Similarly, place all the topping ingredients apart from the pecans in a separate bowl and leave to infuse at room temperature overnight. (With both of these instances, don't worry if you haven't the time to soak the ingredients for that period of time; if you can only manage an hour or so that should allow both to infuse with a good flavour.)

When you are ready for breakfast, preheat the oven to 180°C/350°F/gas mark 4. Place the porridge ingredients in a large heavy-bottomed saucepan and pop over a low heat to slowly cook through. This should take 10–15 minutes; keep stirring as it cooks, adding more milk if necessary. Don't let the porridge angrily bubble, keep it slow and moving – you are aiming for a warm, creamy consistency.

Whilst the porridge is cooking, spread out the pecans on a baking sheet and roast in the oven for about 10 minutes until fragrant and lightly browned. Once cool enough to handle, roughly chop and set aside.

When the porridge is ready and the oats are easily chewable, pour the porridge into bowls. Divide the whiskey-soaked sultanas among the bowls and finish with a good sprinkling of the roasted chopped pecans.

This is my go-to combination for the morning after the night before. It's perfect for perking up any weary guests who may be feeling a little fragile. Folded eggs have a wonderful velvety texture, and adding turmeric really deepens their flavour and accentuates their golden colour. You can use one or two frying pans to make this. If you are working with just one, make sure you have your oven set to a low heat so you can keep the mushrooms and hash browns warm while you cook the eggs. The eggs should be cooked last to make sure you get the best creamy consistency.

# Slow Sunday breakfast

**Serves 4**

*Sweet potato hash browns, miso sweet mushrooms, garlicky spinach and folded golden eggs*

*knob of butter or coconut oil*

*1 garlic clove, crushed*

*200g fresh spinach*

*rye or sourdough bread, toasted, to serve*

*sea salt and black pepper*

**For the hash browns**

*3 large sweet potatoes (or 4 smaller ones), peeled and grated with any liquid squeezed out*

*½ tsp sweet smoked paprika*

*2 eggs, lightly beaten*

*knob of butter or coconut oil*

Begin by preparing the hash browns. Place the grated potato in a medium bowl along with the paprika and a few good grinds of salt and pepper. Give it all a stir before adding the eggs and stirring once again.

Let the mix sit for a minute or so while you heat a frying pan over a high heat. Melt the butter or coconut oil and, using your hands, mould the potato mix into eight small oval-shaped patties. Fry for 6–8 minutes on each side or until you get a nice crispy edge and the potato has cooked through. Use the end of your spatula to flatten down the hash browns slightly as this will help them cook. I usually do four at a time, keeping them warm in a low oven. If you find they are crisping too quickly, reduce the temperature to low and slowly bring it up again.

While the hash browns are sizzling, melt another knob of butter or coconut oil in a second frying pan over a medium heat. Transfer the sliced mushrooms to the pan and give them a quick toss, aiming to brush them each at least slightly with some of the oil. Mushrooms absorb liquids quickly, so work fast. Once they are beginning to gain some heat, add the miso paste and mirin along with 1–2 tablespoons of water – this just helps to loosen the paste. Stir the miso into the mushrooms, giving them all an even and sticky coating.

Continue to cook the mushrooms until they are soft before turning off the heat and leaving them covered so that they don't lose heat.

*For the miso mushrooms*

*about 250g mushrooms (wild, chestnut or Portobello), sliced*

*1 tbsp brown rice miso paste*

*1 tsp mirin (use ½ tsp honey if you can't find it)*

*knob of butter or coconut oil*

*For the folded eggs*

*8 eggs (2 per person)*

*knob of butter or coconut oil*

*½ tsp ground turmeric*

To cook the spinach, melt the coconut oil or butter in a large pan over a low heat, adding the garlic straight away to soften. Tip in all the spinach, packing it down if you need to before placing a lid over to cover. Let it steam for about a minute before giving it all a toss with a wooden spoon and replacing the lid once more. Repeat one or two more times before switching off the heat and leaving it to wilt.

Your hash browns should all be done by now, so you'll have another pan spare. If you are using just one pan, simply transfer the mushrooms to an ovenproof dish and give the pan a little wash to avoid having grey eggs.

In a medium-sized bowl, whisk the eggs along with some salt, pepper and the turmeric. Melt a knob of butter or coconut oil in the frying pan over a medium–high heat and pour in the eggs. Let them sit for about 20 seconds and then, with a relaxed grip on your spatula, fold from the outside in, allowing the egg to flow into the gaps. Cook the eggs to your liking – I like mine quite runny so this takes me about 4 minutes in total.

Serve with the toasted rye or sourdough (and a pot of Earl Grey tea) if you like.

The riper the figs the better this cake, and it works perfectly with any bruised fellows. The overripe fruit has a self-jamming effect, resulting in a wonderfully squidgy cake. I use just a little sugar here as the juicy figs lend a lot of natural sweetness. I like to serve this with some Greek or coconut yoghurt but it is just as delicious as it is and doubles up as a lovely afternoon tea, too.

## Figgy breakfast traybake

**Makes about 16 pieces**

*12 ripe figs*

*200g ground almonds*

*1 tsp baking powder*

*1 tsp ground cinnamon*

*50g light brown soft sugar or coconut sugar*

*zest of 1 orange, juice of ½*

*3 eggs*

*1 tsp vanilla extract*

*60g or 3 good knobs unsalted butter, melted and slightly cooled*

***Equipment***

*Medium-sized ovenproof dish or brownie pan (mine is 20 x 26cm), min. 4cm depth*

Preheat the oven to 180°C/350°F/gas mark 4 and line an ovenproof dish with baking parchment.

Choose the four firmest figs and set them aside. Roughly chop the remaining eight. Don't worry if they are very soft and go a little jammy, that's what we are looking for.

In a large bowl, stir together the ground almonds, baking powder, cinnamon, sugar and orange zest.

In a separate, smaller bowl, whisk the eggs together before adding the vanilla, the orange juice and the melted butter.

Pour the wet mix and the chopped figs into the almond mix and fold to combine. Pour this into the tin and flatten the top with the back of a spoon. Slice the reserved figs and arrange these on the top of the batter.

Bake in the oven for 50–60 minutes or until a wooden skewer inserted into the centre comes out mostly clean with no more than a few crumbs. Remember, there are squishy figs in there so it's a bit of guesswork, but the top should be nicely golden brown and the middle firm.

Allow the cake to cool a little before serving and make sure you let it cool completely before transferring it to an airtight container – it will keep like this for up to 4 days.

# Soups and smalls

I love cooking from scratch, especially when making soups. The flavours always seem to be richer than when they are shop-bought and it can often be a great way to use up any leftover vegetables. There is nothing more comforting than plunging a spoon into a bowl of hot homemade soup, and I find the process of making it quite cathartic too. The recipes in this chapter can be enjoyed as a light lunch, a snack to fill the gap or as a starter to the main event.

As a general rule I try to eat as seasonally and locally as I can. I've mentioned in the introductions to each recipe whether they're more fitting for the cooler months and those which are best enjoyed during the summer. Of course you can swap and change as you wish, but I do find that the ingredients taste best when in season.

Bright, bold and earthy, beetroot is one of the vegetables I still marvel at. In winter they are delicious roasted but when the weather is warmer I adore blitzing them into this refreshing soup. It is perfect for when you have lots of guests as it can be made ahead, requiring no heating time. I prefer to boil my beetroot at home for this, as the flavour is so much sweeter, but if you are pushed for time you can use pre-packed, vacuum-sealed beetroots – just choose a brand that doesn't have too high a vinegar content, as this can leave rather a sharp taste.

## Beetroot, cucumber and mint gazpacho

**Serves 8**

*8–10 medium beets, boiled for about 20 minutes, skins removed and cooled*

*½ red onion, roughly chopped*

*2 garlic cloves, smashed with the back of a knife*

*1 large cucumber, roughly chopped*

*bunch of mint leaves, roughly chopped, plus extra finely chopped leaves, to serve*

*6 tbsp olive oil, plus extra (optional)*

*3 tbsp sherry vinegar or red wine vinegar, plus extra (optional)*

*750ml ice-cold water*

*sea salt and black pepper*

***Optional toppings***

*toasted seeds, finely sliced avocado, diced cucumber, olive oil, Greek yoghurt or coconut yoghurt*

Place all the soup ingredients into a blender and blend on high speed until very smooth. Taste and add more salt, pepper, sherry vinegar or olive oil, if needed.

Transfer to a bowl and keep in the fridge until ready to serve.

Serve sprinkled with some freshly chopped mint, if you like, and ground black pepper or your toppings of choice.

Tip: if you are boiling your own beetroot and are left with the stems, try simply sautéing them in a pan. Separate the stems from the leaves and roughly chop both. Add some butter or coconut oil, grated ginger and garlic to a pan, followed by the stems, frying on a medium heat for about 2 minutes before adding the leaves. Cook until the leaves are wilted and serve right away.

This is a great way to use up any sad-looking vegetables. This soup works wonderfully with either broccoli or carrots, and the cashews add a lovely creaminess that is incredibly comforting on a wintery day. If you have a high-speed, powerful blender there is no need to soak the nuts, which really makes this quick to whip up.

# Hot-shot carrot or broccoli, ginger, lemongrass and cashew soup

**Serves 4**

*500g broccoli or carrots, roughly chopped (about 1 small head of broccoli including the stalk or a small bunch of carrots)*

*handful of raw, unsalted cashew nuts*

*1 lemongrass stick*

*thumb-sized piece of ginger*

*1/2 chilli, deseeded (optional) and chopped*

*1 small garlic clove or 1/2 large one, crushed through a garlic crusher or finely chopped*

*sea salt and black pepper*

**To serve**

*coriander and Toasted seeds (see pages 244–5)*

*Savoury oat and buckwheat granola (see page 222)*

If you have a high-speed blender such as a Vitamix, simply throw all the ingredients into the blending jug with 500ml boiling hot water and turn the dial from low to high before flicking the intensity switch to intense for 2–3 minutes until you have a smooth creamy consistency and the soup is warmed to your liking. If you prefer a thinner soup, add a little more water.

If you are using a stick blender or normal blender, place all the ingredients, including the cashews, into a large saucepan with 750ml boiling hot water and bring to the boil. Reduce the heat and allow it all simmer until the carrots or broccoli are soft. This should take 6–7 minutes for the broccoli and 15 for the carrots. Once tender, transfer everything to a blender and whizz until you have a smooth and creamy soup, or if you are using a stick blender keep it all in the pan and whizz. For a thinner soup, simply add a little more water.

If you'd like a little more heat to the soup, using either of the above methods reheat slowly in a pan before serving up and finishing off with a sprinkling of the coriander and crunchy seeds, or the savoury granola.

This is one of those soups that immediately makes me feel better. It is thick and creamy with a deep nutty flavour that gives it a toasty cosiness. I like to make big vats of this and freeze it in batches so that it is ready for those rainy days when all I want to do is indulge in a good soak while dinner bubbles effortlessly on the hob. I love making use of the whole pumpkin including the seeds, keeping any extra in a little jar for snacking on.

## Pumpkin, parsnip and almond butter soup

**10 portions**

*with toasted pumpkin seeds and coconut*

*About 1.5kg pumpkin or butternut squash, seeds removed and reserved, flesh chopped into chunks*

*500g parsnips, peeled and chopped in half*

*about 4 tbsp melted coconut oil or olive oil*

*good pinch of sea salt*

*handful of unsweetened flaked coconut*

*1 onion, finely chopped*

*4 garlic cloves*

*½ tsp ground cinnamon*

*1 tsp ground coriander*

*generous grind of black pepper*

*2 litres homemade chicken or vegetable stock (or organic stock cube)*

*6 heaped tbsp almond butter (palm-oil free)*

*coriander leaves, to serve (optional)*

Preheat the oven to 180°C/350°F/gas mark 4.

Tip the pumpkin or squash chunks into a roasting tin with the parsnips, drizzle with the oil and roast in the oven for 40 minutes or until soft.

While the vegetables are roasting, prepare the seeds and coconut. Give the reserved seeds a good wash under a cold tap to try to remove as much of the flesh as you can. Don't worry if you cannot get rid of it all – the little stringy bits add a wonderful crunch.

Once the seeds are mostly flesh-free, pat them dry with some paper towel and toss them in a little melted coconut oil and sea salt before roasting them in the oven below the pumpkin or squash for about 15–20 minutes or until dry and crunchy.

Transfer the seeds to a plate and allow them to cool before sprinkling the coconut flakes over the same tray you used for the seeds and placing them in the oven below the vegetables. Let the flakes toast for about 5 minutes but watch them all the time as they can easily burn. Allow to cool and set aside with the seeds until you are ready to serve.

Once the vegetables are cooked, heat a further tablespoon of coconut oil in a large pot or pan and add the onion, garlic and spices to soften and leave the flavours to infuse. I like to add a few tablespoons of water to prevent the garlic burning.

Once the onion is soft, add the stock and roasted pumpkin and parsnips, salt, pepper and finally the almond butter. Bring the temperature to a medium heat and let everything cook for 5–10 minutes before blending with a stick blender. If you don't have a stick blender you can transfer the soup into a blender in batches. Add more water if you want to loosen the soup.

Heat the soup and ladle into bowls, then serve sprinkled with the toasted pumpkin seeds and coconut. If you have any coriander lying around this makes a wonderful garnish, too.

When the evenings are cold and I am tired after work, all I crave is a warm bowl of food, simple but not boring. This one-pot curry soup is perfect for those moments and takes less than half an hour to put together. When my nose is running with winter cold, a big bowl of this, spiked with fresh chilli for a real zing, warms me from the inside out. The chilli is not essential, though, and the curry itself has more of a subtle spice mainly from the ginger and lemongrass. It's also great to make when you are entertaining. You can prepare the base ingredients ahead of time then just nip to the kitchen to finish it off fifteen minutes or so before you plan to sit down.

# Hake, prawn and lemongrass curry soup

**Serves 4–6**

*1 tbsp coconut oil*

*1 onion, finely chopped*

*large bunch of coriander, leaves and stems separated, plus extra to serve*

*thumb-sized piece of ginger, peeled and finely chopped*

*2 garlic cloves, crushed or finely chopped*

*2 lemongrass stalks, finely chopped*

*1 tsp ground coriander*

*½ tsp ground turmeric*

*1 tsp coriander seeds*

*400ml tin coconut milk*

*1 red pepper, deseeded and sliced*

*400g hake fillets, cut into 8–12 pieces*

*300g peeled prawns*

*handful of mangetout*

*juice of 1 lime, plus wedges to serve*

*cooked rice and chopped fresh chilli to serve (optional)*

Melt the coconut oil in a wide, deep frying pan, then add the onion and cook for about 5 minutes to soften, adding a few tablespoons of water if it is browning too quickly.

Meanwhile, finely chop the coriander stems and half of the leaves, reserving the rest for garnishing. Add the chopped coriander, ginger, garlic, lemongrass, ground coriander, turmeric and whole coriander seeds to the onion and stir to combine, creating a chunky base for the curry. Once everything has begun to cook and smell fragrant, add the coconut milk and sliced pepper, bring everything to a simmer and cook for about 5 minutes to infuse the flavour.

Gently add the hake fillets to the curry sauce, dot the prawns evenly between the fish and sprinkle over the mangetout. Squeeze over the lime juice, cover the pan with a lid and cook for about 8 minutes until the prawns are opaque and the fish is cooked through – the flesh should be opaque and it should flake easily.

Taste the curry for seasoning and serve in bowls with the cooked rice, if using. Scatter over the remaining coriander leaves and chili, if you like, and serve with lime wedges to squeeze over.

Wasabi is the perfect match for buttery smooth salmon, and the combination of pink and green looks wonderful on the plate. I don't think the artist in me will ever get bored of the colours in this salad. A perfect summer dish, it makes for a delicious light main course too. This is a great stress-free option for a dinner party; the salmon can be cooked in advance and the courgettes and lettuce can be prepared and kept in the fridge until needed.

# Bang-bang wasabi salmon salad

**Serves 4**

*2 salmon fillets, preferably skin off*

***Salad***

*2 courgettes*

*1 gem lettuce, shredded*

*2 tsp toasted sesame oil*

*2 tbsp raw apple cider vinegar*

*pinch of sea salt*

*1 birds eye chilli, deseeded and finely chopped*

*2 heaped tbsp finely chopped mint, plus extra to serve (optional)*

***Dressing***

*1 avocado, stoned and peeled*

*1 tbsp tahini*

*2 tbsp raw apple cider vinegar*

*2 tsp wasabi paste, or to taste*

*cont.*

Preheat the oven to 190°C/375°F/gas mark 5.

First, cook the salmon. Lightly oil a baking tray and cook the fillets, skin-side down if they have skin, for 10–12 minutes. Once cooked, remove the salmon and allow to cool completely. If the salmon has skin, remove it now, if you like. I like to lightly brush both sides of the removed skin with some oil and sprinkle a little salt on it before placing it back under the grill and munching on it like a crisp. You can also serve it as a fancy crisp on top of the salad.

While the salmon cools, prepare the salad. Begin by grating the courgettes and, in handfuls, squeeze out as much of their liquid as you can over the sink – they have a high water content, so this prevents a soggy salad. Place the squeezed courgette into a medium bowl and add the sesame oil, cider vinegar, salt, chopped chilli and mint. Toss everything together, set aside or place in the fridge for the flavours to infuse while you get on with the dressing.

Place the avocado, tahini, cider vinegar, wasabi paste, sea salt and half the water into a food processor and blend until smooth. Add the remaining water (and more if needed) until you reach the desired consistency. It's completely up to your preference – I like my dressing the consistency of thick Greek yoghurt so it's easy to scoop up with the salmon.

cont.

*pinch of sea salt*

*8 tbsp cold water*

*a handful of toasted seeds (pages 244–245, optional)*

Once everything is prepared and the salmon has cooled, flake the fish. You'll notice that it naturally has a few lines running through it, which I think resemble waves. Using a knife and fork, gently go along these lines and separate the 'waves' of salmon. Take your time and don't panic if it doesn't look overly neat. You'll probably find that there are a few scrappy bits – you can place these on the salad first and easily disguise them with the neat flakes.

To build your salad, start by placing a good handful of the shredded lettuce onto the plates followed by about two handfuls of the courgette and finally place the salmon – scrappy bits first! – on top. Then drizzle or spoon over your dressing and finally top with shredded mint and seeds, if you are using them.

This is a relatively basic soup recipe which contains just three ingredients. Although subtle, the miso brings a wonderful sweetness to the soup that, paired with fragrant garlic, really brings it to life. I like to eat this when I am feeling slightly run-down and tired, which is just perfect as you could almost make it with your eyes closed. Be sure not to waste the leaves, but keep these aside for later – fried in a wok with a little ginger, chilli and tamari, they make a wonderful side dish.

# White miso and cauliflower soup

*with toasted sunflower seeds*

**Serves 4**

*2–3 medium heads of cauliflower, chopped into 5cm chunks*

*1 large garlic clove*

*4 heaped tbsp white miso paste*

*sea salt and black pepper*

***To serve***

*Toasted flaked almonds or seeds (pages 244–5)*

Tip the chopped cauliflower into a large saucepan with just enough water to cover. Using the flat edge of the knife and the heel of your hand, smash the garlic clove and peel off the skin before adding the whole clove to the cauliflower. Bring to the boil and simmer until the cauliflower is soft enough that you can pierce it with a table knife – about 15 minutes. I place a lid over the saucepan, slightly ajar, and check it every 5 minutes or so to make sure the water hasn't all evaporated. If this does happen, just add more. Don't let the cauliflower drown in water, though – the idea is to let it steam.

When the cauliflower is tender, remove the lid and let it cool slightly before pouring out the water into a mug and leaving about a mug's worth in the saucepan.

Add the miso paste and, either with your stick blender or in a food processor, blend until smooth, gradually adding the reserved water until you reach your desired consistency.

Season to taste and reheat slowly over a medium heat. Transfer to individual bowls and serve, topped with a good handful of toasted almonds or seeds.

One of the best meals I had while in Morocco was on a rooftop overlooking Marrakesh. They had a seasonal menu and most of what was cooked was grown by the restaurant owners themselves. There are two salads which still stick in my memory today; one was a delicious spiced fennel dish and the other a wonderfully sweet candied walnut and chicory salad. Almost an amalgam of them both, this recipe marries the two tastes and is incredibly easy to make. It can be served warm or cold, which is particularly nice during summer. I love to use a griddle pan to achieve that wonderful charred effect but a standard frying pan will work too.

## Charred fennel, chicory and fig salad

*with a sweet ginger dressing*

**Serves 4**

*4 chicory heads, sliced in half lengthways*

*2 fennel bulbs, sliced into about 2cm slices*

*about 3 tbsp olive oil*

*juice of ½ lemon*

*6–8 small fresh figs (about 400g)*

*sea salt and black pepper*

*50g pecans or walnuts, toasted (see page 245) and chopped, to serve*

***For the dressing***

*1–2 tbsp balsamic vinegar*

*4 tbsp walnut or cold-pressed olive oil*

*3 tbsp pomegranate molasses*

*1 tsp wholegrain mustard*

*thumb-sized piece of ginger, peeled and grated*

Rub the chopped chicory and fennel in the oil before heating a large frying pan or griddle pan. When the pan is hot, arrange the chicory and fennel and cook for about 10 minutes, turning halfway. Squeeze over the lemon juice and allow it to cook for a further minute either side.

Meanwhile, quarter or finely slice the firmest 3–4 figs and set aside. Chop the riper figs as small as you can – ideally they will break slightly, creating a self-jamming effect.

To make the dressing, place the ingredients in a small bowl and whisk with a fork. Add the slightly jammy figs and whisk again until you have a chunky fruity dressing.

When the fennel and chicory are done, transfer them either to plates or a large serving dish. Spoon over the dressing and top with the sliced figs and chopped pecans or walnuts.

One of my favourite things about autumn is its colours – the vibrant red, orange and yellow – so it seems perfectly appropriate that the vegetables of the season should echo these. This recipe uses acorn squash (one of my favourites) for its bold nutty flavour and contrasting green skin that looks fantastic when cooked. I have teamed it with a zesty avocado cream but it also goes beautifully with some feta crumbled over the top. Although I prefer to eat this dish warm it is also delicious cold, so don't be afraid to make extra and store it in the fridge for Sunday night suppers – it's perfect for leftovers.

# Roasted acorn squash

*with herby oil, toasted squash seeds and lemon avocado cream*

**Serves 4–6**

***For the squash***

*2–3 acorn squash (depending on size)*

*rapeseed or olive oil, for roasting (about 3 tbsp)*

*sea salt and freshly ground black pepper*

*spices of choice – mixed spice, chilli (optional)*

***For the herby oil***

*handful of basil leaves*

*large handful of coriander leaves*

*smaller handful of parsley leaves*

*6 tbsp cold-pressed olive oil, plus extra (optional)*

*1 large garlic clove, crushed*

*zest of 1 lemon*

*sea salt and black pepper to taste*

Preheat oven to 180°C/350°F/gas mark 4.

Chop the squash into roughly 1cm slices, leaving the skin on, and remove the seeds, placing them in a colander. Rinse the seeds under cold running water and, using your hands, try to remove as much of the pulp as you can. Don't be too precious about this – the roasted pulp has a wonderful caramelised flavour and adds more of a rustic look to the dish.

Pat dry the seeds with kitchen paper, sprinkle with a little oil and season with salt and pepper. You can also include a few spices here, if you like – I occasionally add a pinch of mixed spice and chilli.

Place the seeds on a baking tray and roast in the oven for 15–20 minutes, checking and tossing every few minutes to make sure they are not burning. Set aside to cool.

While the seeds cool, cook the squash. Season and oil the squash slices and place on a lightly oiled baking tray, then transfer to the oven for 30–35 minutes or until they have got a bit of colour and can be pierced easily with a fork.

To make the herby oil, blitz all the ingredients in a food processor. If you don't have one, do this by hand and simply finely chop the herbs before mixing with the rest of the ingredients. Feel free to be creative with your herbs and the ratios you use – my suggestion here is just a guideline.

***For the lemon avocado cream***

*2 ripe avocados, stoned and peeled*

*juice of 1–2 lemons (depending on how zingy you like it)*

*pinch of sea salt*

To make the lemon avocado cream, blitz the ingredients in a food processor until you have a smooth and creamy consistency. It will be a little tricky to do this without a food processor but if your avocado is ripe enough you should be able to get a smooth cream by first smashing and then whisking with a fork.

Once the squash is cooked, arrange the slices on individual plates or one large plate. Drizzle over a generous amount of the herby oil followed by the toasted seeds and serve with the lemon avocado cream, either on the side or spooned over.

I love using simple vegetables as the star of the table. This recipe turns the humble white cabbage into a bit of a showstopper, with just a little attention to seasoning and some good herbs. My favourite herb combination for this is mint and basil; it gives it a real zing and tastes wonderfully fresh.

# Roasted cabbage steaks

*with herby yoghurt and toasted pecans*

**Serves 4**

*1 large head of white cabbage*

*drizzle of cold-pressed extra virgin olive oil*

*small handful of pecans*

***For the dressing***

*about 4 tbsp butter or coconut oil, melted, plus extra for greasing*

*3 tbsp balsamic vinegar*

*2 tbsp honey or maple syrup*

*1 garlic clove, crushed or finely chopped*

*sea salt and black pepper*

Preheat the oven to 200°C/400°F/gas mark 6 and lightly grease a large baking tray.

Begin by removing any tough outer leaves from the cabbage and reserve these for a stock or slaw (see page 124), if you like. Sit the cabbage on its base and slice it at two ends to create flat edges. Then slice the cabbage evenly into four roughly 2cm-thick 'steaks'.

In a small bowl, mix the butter or oil, balsamic vinegar, honey or maple syrup, garlic and a few grinds of salt and pepper until combined.

Arrange the cabbage steaks on the baking tray and with a pastry brush paint the dressing lightly over each of the steaks before turning them and painting over the other side. Go more generously on the second side as much of the glaze will seep towards the bottom during cooking. If you don't have a pastry brush to hand you can also use a teaspoon for this and just spread the glaze as evenly as you can.

Place the cabbage steaks in the oven and roast for about 25 minutes before flipping them over and continuing to roast for a further 25 minutes or until they are nicely browned with crispy edges.

To toast the pecans, simply tip them onto an ungreased baking tray and place in the oven with the cabbage for 10 minutes. Remove once they have taken on some colour and are beginning to smell fragrant. Allow them to cool for a few minutes before roughly chopping and setting aside.

*For the herby yoghurt*

*handful of fresh mint, coriander, basil, or a mix*

*4 tbsp full-fat Greek yoghurt or coconut yoghurt*

*zest of ½ lemon (plus a little juice for squeezing)*

*pinch of sea salt*

To make the herby yoghurt, finely chop the herbs before mixing them with the yoghurt, lemon zest and a pinch of salt.

Once the cabbage steaks are ready, plate them up with a drizzle of cold-pressed olive oil, a squeeze of lemon and a spoonful of the herby yoghurt. Finish with a generous sprinkle of the toasted pecans and serve.

These fritters are a brilliant snack or starter when you have guests over as they can be made into bite-sized pieces and enjoyed without the need for a knife and fork. They're also lovely made a little bigger and served as a pre-dinner starter. I love to serve these with some sliced avocado or my quick Avocado and yellow pepper smash (page 180) and a good spoonful of chutney.

# Spiced sweetcorn fritters

*with quick beetroot chutney*

**Serves 4–6**

*500g cooked sweetcorn kernels*

*2 large eggs*

*1 tsp ground turmeric*

*½ tsp ground cumin*

*pinch of cayenne pepper*

*60g white spelt or coconut flour*

*1 tsp baking powder*

*butter, coconut or rapeseed oil, for frying*

*sea salt and black pepper*

***For the chutney***

*2–3 boiled and peeled beetroots, roughly chopped*

*1 large eating apple, chopped into ½cm pieces*

*70g sultanas*

*3 tbsp red wine vinegar*

*4 tbsp light brown soft sugar or coconut sugar*

*zest of 1 orange*

First make the chutney. Add the chopped beetroot to the pan along with the apple, sultanas, red wine vinegar, sugar, orange zest and 2 tablespoons of water and heat over a low heat for 10–15 minutes, stirring gently. Transfer to a clean bowl or jar – if you are not using this immediately it will keep, covered, in the fridge for up to three days.

Divide the sweetcorn in half and tip one half into the food processor. Add the eggs, some salt and pepper, the spices, flour and baking powder and process until smooth. Add the remaining corn and pulse just a few times to break up the remaining kernels slightly but still ensuring that there is texture.

Heat the butter or oil in a non-stick pan over a medium heat and drop about 2 tablespoons of the fritter mix into the pan. I tend to cook about 3 fritters at once. Fry for 3–4 minutes on each side, adding more butter or oil to the pan between each batch. Make sure the pan isn't too hot or your fritters will burn. If you'd like to make bite-sized fritters, use about 2 teaspoons of the mix instead of tablespoons and fry them for about 2 minutes on each side. Serve with the chutney on the side.

I call this a busy courgette salad as it's a great one for when you are super busy because it can be thrown together in minutes. Don't forget to squeeze out the moisture from the courgette or else you will have a slightly wet salad. Feel free to use whichever nuts and nut butter you have to hand – cashews and cashew butter also make a delicious combination.

## Hot and spicy prawn skewers

*with busy courgette and peanut salad*

**Serves 4**

*1 tsp dried chilli flakes*

*½ tsp cayenne pepper*

*1 tsp toasted sesame oil*

*1 tbsp lemon juice*

*1 tbsp olive oil*

*1 small garlic clove, crushed*

*16 large prawns, peeled and heads removed*

*sea salt and black pepper*

*coconut or rapeseed oil, for frying*

*4 skewers*

***For the courgette salad***

*70g raw peanuts*

*3 tbsp crunchy peanut butter*

*1 tsp sesame oil*

*2 tbsp apple cider vinegar*

*2 tbsp cold-pressed olive oil*

*2 courgettes, grated and juices squeezed out*

*handful of coriander or basil, roughly chopped*

If you are using wooden skewers, begin by soaking them in lukewarm water for about 30 minutes to ensure that the wood doesn't burn or splinter when over the heat.

Place the peanuts in a large pan over a medium heat and toast them for about 10 minutes, tossing frequently. If the peanuts have skin, don't worry too much if this starts burning a little. When the nuts have gained some nice colour and smell fragrant, transfer them to a dry tea towel or cloth and rub them vigorously to remove their skins. Then transfer them to a plate and allow them to cool before roughly chopping.

For the prawn skewers, place the chilli flakes, cayenne pepper, sesame oil, lemon juice, olive oil, garlic and salt and pepper in a small bowl and mix to combine. Add the prawns and coat in the marinade using your hands. Set aside for 10 minutes to allow the flavours to infuse.

Meanwhile, get on with the salad. Combine the peanut butter, sesame oil, vinegar and olive oil in a medium bowl and season to taste. Add the courgette, coriander or basil and peanuts and toss together using two spoons.

Thread the prawns evenly onto four skewers – you should have four per skewer. Heat a teaspoon of oil in a griddle pan over a high heat. Cook the prawn skewers for just 2–3 minutes either side until they are opaque.

Divide the salad evenly among four individual plates and place the hot spicy prawns alongside. Serve straight away.

This is broccoli well and truly dressed, and it is one of my favourite dinner-party dishes. Brown shrimps may seem a bit of an unusual choice but they add a wonderful flavour. I am a bit of a traditionalist so I always use butter here but olive oil works fine, too. The salsa is punchy and it marries perfectly with the smooth lemony sauce. Serve it in a big bowl with lots of little plates and a good loaf of bread as the buttery sauce is delicious for dipping into.

# Tenderstem broccoli

*with lemon-buttered brown shrimps and salsa verde*

**Serves 4–5**

*about 75g butter*

*1 tbsp good-quality Dijon mustard*

*zest and juice of 1 lemon*

*about 400g Tenderstem broccoli*

*90g brown shrimps*

**For the salsa verde**

*1 large bunch of basil, leaves and stems*

*leaves of 1 bunch of parsley*

*handful of mint leaves*

*1 tbsp capers*

*1 garlic clove, crushed or finely chopped*

*3 tbsp red wine vinegar*

*zest and juice of 1 lemon*

*6 tbsp cold-pressed olive oil*

*sea salt and black pepper*

Begin by making the salsa. I like a coarse, uneven salsa. Finely chop the herbs and add to a bowl with the capers, garlic, red wine vinegar, lemon zest and juice and olive oil. Stir well and season to taste. If you are pushed for time you could blitz everything in a food processor.

Next, melt the butter in a small saucepan over a medium heat until it begins to foam a little and brown. Remove from the heat and add the mustard, lemon zest and juice, whisking together with a fork. (You can use olive oil instead of butter, if you like, in which case simply skip the heating process and whisk everything together in a small bowl.)

Bring a medium–large saucepan full of water to the boil. Add a good pinch of salt and boil the broccoli for about 3 minutes until cooked but still al dente. Drain in a colander.

Pour the lemon-butter sauce into the large pan, add the shrimps and cook for about 1 minute or just until warm. Add the broccoli to the pan and gently toss it to coat it in the lemony shrimp sauce.

Transfer to a serving dish and spoon over the salsa verde. Any extra salsa can be served in a small bowl on the side to dip bread into or kept in the fridge for later – it is delicious served with fish or stirred into rice or pasta.

These fish cakes are best served hot out of the pan alongside the chilled cucumber salad. I like to prepare the cucumber a few hours ahead so that it has more of a pickle to it. There is the option to add a little spice, too, which plays well against the coolness of the cucumber, but you can omit the cayenne if you have a more sensitive palate. I use rapeseed oil for the dressing over olive as it has a milder taste.

# Thai pollock fish cakes

*with quick sesame pickled cucumbers and chilli zing sauce*

**Serves 4–6**

*1 lemongrass stalk, outer leaves removed and finely chopped*

*1 large garlic clove, crushed or finely chopped*

*thumb-sized piece of ginger, peeled and roughly chopped*

*2 spring onions, finely chopped,*

*1 red chilli, deseeded and roughly chopped*

*1 bunch of coriander, stems and leaves roughly chopped*

*400g pollock or other white fish, such as cod or haddock*

*zest and juice of 1 lime*

*2 tsp toasted sesame oil*

*1 tbsp fish sauce (or just use tamari or soy sauce)*

*1 egg, lightly beaten*

*coconut oil, for frying*

I recommend making the cucumber salad first to give the cucumbers time to marinate – the longer you can leave them the better they taste.

Slice your cucumbers in half lengthways. Then, using a teaspoon, scrape out the watery centre (I like to throw this into smoothies) before finely slicely into crescent-shaped pieces.

In a medium bowl, whisk together the remaining salad ingredients, apart from the sesame seeds, and add the cucumber, tossing until combined. Chill until ready to serve, then just before serving drain the excess liquid before adding the sesame seeds.

To make the chilli zing sauce, simply whisk all the ingredients in a small bowl using a fork and allow to infuse at room temperature for 1 hour. If you are making it a day ahead let the dressing infuse in the fridge.

To make the fish cakes, put the lemongrass, garlic, ginger, spring onions, chilli and coriander into your food processor and pulse for about 30 seconds or until well broken down. Add the fish, lime zest and juice, toasted sesame oil, fish sauce and egg and blend until you have a smooth paste. Transfer the fish mix to a bowl, cover and chill in the fridge for 15–20 minutes or until the mix has firmed up a little.

Using your hands, shape the mix into 16 patties. Melt a little coconut oil in a frying pan and fry the fish cakes for 3–4 minutes on each side until golden and cooked through.

*For the seasame pickled cucumber salad*

*2 large cucumbers*

*2 pinches of salt*

*4 tbsp Japanese rice wine vinegar or apple cider vinegar*

*1 tbsp toasted sesame oil*

*1 tbsp mirin (if you don't have it use 1 tsp honey and 1 extra tsp vinegar)*

*1 tsp tamari*

*2 tbsp toasted sesame seeds*

*For the chilli zing sauce*

*1 chilli, deseeded (optional) and very finely chopped*

*½ garlic clove, crushed or finely chopped*

*1 tbsp rice wine vinegar*

*½ tbsp light brown soft sugar or coconut sugar*

*1 tbsp toasted sesame oil*

*4 tbs tamari or soy sauce*

*juice of 1 lime*

*½ bunch of coriander leaves, finely chopped (keep the rest of the bunch to garnish)*

To serve, either divide the pickled cucumber salad among plates and top each with two or three fish cakes or arrange as above on a larger scale on a serving dish. Sprinkle with a few roughly chopped coriander leaves and place the chilli zing sauce in a small bowl for people to either pour over or dip in.

There are days when I like to spend hours in the kitchen but there are also those when I want something quick, wholesome and delicious on the table without any fuss – and ideally with little or no washing up! This is a recipe for those times. A bit of a twist on classic mussels, these are spiked with ginger and saffron. The golden saffron and turmeric give it a warming depth as well as fantastic colour. Watch your clothes and I would even advise tucking your napkin into your shirt, as the soupy cooking liquid is good enough to slurp.

# Saffron, coconut mussels

*with ginger and coriander*

**Serves 4**

*2 tbsp coconut oil*

*2 shallots, finely chopped*

*2 garlic cloves, crushed, or finely chopped*

*thumb-sized (or larger) piece of ginger, peeled and finely chopped*

*good pinch of saffron threads*

*1 tsp turmeric*

*pinch of cayenne pepper*

*½ tsp sea salt*

*400ml tin full-fat coconut milk*

*1 'tin' fish or vegetable stock (use the tin from the milk)*

*½ 'tin' dry white wine (or more stock)*

*about 1kg mussels, scrubbed and debearded*

*juice of 1 lime*

*handful of chopped coriander, to serve*

Place the coconut oil, shallots and garlic in a very large pot over a low–medium heat and cook until softened and slightly browned. Add the ginger, saffron, turmeric, cayenne pepper and salt and cook for another minute, stirring as you do.

Pour in the coconut milk, stock and wine, if you like, using the tin from the coconut milk to measure, and allow the liquid to come to the boil. Once it has started to bubble, tip in the mussels, stirring them to ensure they are coated in the sauce. Place the lid on the pan, reduce the heat and simmer the mussels for 7–9 minutes or until they have opened up – discard any that haven't opened.

Turn off the heat and add the lime juice and half of the coriander. Ladle into serving bowl and sprinkle with the remaining coriander.

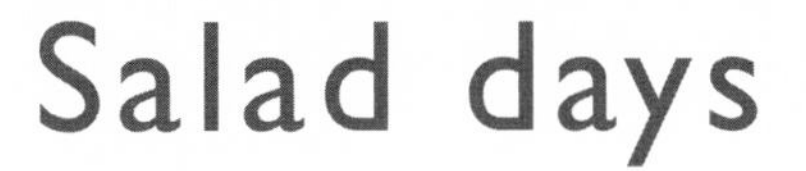

# Salad days

For me, the word salad means anything but a soggy bowl of lettuce. A good dressing is often the key ingredient to making a salad sing. I am of the belief that almost anything can be brought to life with the right seasoning and a little dressing up and I am a big believer in using up leftovers, as often these can be turned into the most wonderful salads. Roasted sweet potatoes from Sunday lunch often become my Moroccan sweet potato salad (page 80) and any slightly floppy vegetables that have been forgotten at the back of the fridge will be brought back to life again in my Sad vegetable salad (page 86). Some of these salads can be enjoyed warm, too, and all of them will keep for a few days in the fridge or can be tossed into Tupperware to create a delicious lunch on the go.

Mojo verde is a rather fantastic translation of green sauce. It originally comes from the Canary Islands, where it was traditionally made with local green peppers or pimenta. Other countries developed their own variation of the sauce, some using just herbs or adding chunks of stale bread and handfuls of spices. I have tasted many but this is my favourite version, which uses mainly olive oil and herbs. The tarragon adds a lovely aromatic taste here and the ground coriander provides an extra kick. The mojo verde will keep for about a week in the fridge, so I often make double as it is a great way to liven up some simply grilled chicken or fish.

# Roasted new potatoes, green beans

*and tarragon mojo verde*

**Serves 8–10**

*1kg new potatoes*

*about 2 tbsp rapeseed or olive oil*

*500g green beans*

*sea salt and black pepper*

***For the tarragon mojo verde***

*4 garlic cloves, crushed*

*handful of tarragon leaves, roughly chopped*

*large bunch of coriander, stems chopped small, leaves roughly chopped*

*½ tsp ground coriander*

*1 tbsp lemon juice*

*1 tbsp apple cider vinegar*

*100ml cold-pressed olive oil*

Preheat the oven to 200°C/400°F/gas mark 6.

Chop any larger new potatoes in half so that they are all roughly the same size, then place them in a large roasting tray. Drizzle them with a good coating of oil and sprinkle over a decent pinch of sea salt and freshly ground pepper. Roast until cooked through and crispy – this should take about 45–50 minutes. After about 35 minutes, check them; if you feel they are nearly there, add the green beans for the last 15 minutes; if not, cook a little longer before adding the beans.

To make the mojo verde, transfer the garlic, tarragon, fresh and ground coriander, lemon juice and cider vinegar to a food processor with some salt and pepper and pulse until well broken down – use a spatula to push the mix down and whizz again to make sure it is all evenly blended. With the motor running, gradually drizzle in the olive oil until the mojo verde reaches a pesto-like consistency.

Transfer the potatoes and beans to a large dish and drizzle over about three-quarters of the mojo verde. Give everything a good toss before loosely drizzling the rest of the mojo verde over the salad. This salad will keep for about 3 days in the fridge.

I'm a big fan of getting my vegetables from as close to the earth as I can and if I haven't grown them myself I tend to buy them from local markets or vegetable stalls. That way you get all that the vegetable has to offer. Some people like to cut off the stalky bits of leaves but often I find these the best bits. This recipe celebrates every part of the beetroot; the sweet purple bulb, the salty crunchy stems and the rich green leaves. It's an incredibly comforting salad which can be enjoyed both warm or cold.

# Beet stem, bulb and leaf salad

*with toasted sunflower seeds*

**Serves 4**

*about 6 beetroot*

*about 200g kale*

*olive oil, for frying*

*about 70g toasted sunflower seeds (see page 244)*

***For the dressing***

*5 tbsp cold-pressed olive oil*

*zest of 1 lemon*

*1 tbsp lemon juice*

*1 tbsp apple cider vinegar*

*1 tsp tamari*

*1 tsp toasted sesame oil*

*2 tbsp pomegranate molasses*

Preheat the oven to 200°C/400°F/gas mark 6.

Separate the beetroot bulbs from their stems and trim off any very tough-looking areas from the skin, then wash and give them a good scrub with a vegetable brush to remove the dirt. Do the same for the stems, this time removing the tough base part as well as any straggly or slightly unhappy-looking stems or leaves. Wash well and drain in a colander.

Cut the beet bulbs in half, then cut each half into three wedges. Spread them out in a large roasting dish, skin and rounded side down.

Roast for 30–40 minutes or until they have begun to shrivel from their skins and char slightly. You may find some even bubble a little as they begin to release some of their natural sweetness.

Once the bulbs are roasted, switch off the oven and leave them inside to keep warm while you get on with the rest of the vegetables. You may want to keep the door slightly ajar at the start to avoid them overcooking, then close it as the oven starts to cool.

Trim the stems from the leaves of the beet stems before chopping the stem bits into roughly 1cm pieces. Set aside and roughly chop the remaining beetroot leaves with the kale leaves, removing any very woody stems (keep these for stock).

Splash about 1 tablespoon of olive oil into a frying pan and throw in the beet stems, keeping them moving to coat them in oil. Cook the stems on a medium heat for 2 minutes until they have gained a little softness but are not fully cooked.

Add the beet leaves, kale and about 2 tablespoons of water and continue to stir-fry for a further 4–5 minutes until the leaves are wilted and have darkened in colour. The water just helps the vegetables to steam a little.

In a large bowl, combine all the dressing ingredients and whisk using a fork before transferring the leaves and stems, roasted beetroot and most of the sunflower seeds to the bowl and giving everything a good toss.

Either pile up the salad on individual plates or onto a serving dish and sprinkle with a few more toasted sunflower seeds, then serve straight away.

I love using avocado to make a dressing; with a little fresh lime juice for a bit of a tang it makes for a wonderfully creamy and zesty finish. Fresh broad beans work best for this salad, but if you can't find them or they are out of season, frozen are good too. I like to wash the radish leaves and dress them in a simple olive oil and Dijon mustard dressing (see page 13) to act as another little salad side, or you could use them to make my Radish leaf pesto (see page 136) and keep it in a jar in the fridge for another time.

## Broad bean, radish and avocado salad

**Serves 4–6**

*bunch of radishes (about 200g)*

*500g podded broad beans, blanched for 2 minutes (or blanched from frozen)*

*3 tbsp cold-pressed olive oil*

*zest of 2 limes and juice of 1–2 depending on how citrusy you like it*

*2 avocados*

*1–2 tbsp finely shredded herbs – mint or coriander work best*

*sea salt and black pepper*

Wash the radishes, cut off the leaves, then finely slice the roots and place them directly into your serving bowl.

Add the broad beans, olive oil, lime zest and the juice of 1 lime. Cut the avocados in half, remove the stones and scoop out the flesh – there is no need to be neat when doing this as it will get mushed up anyway. Then using your hands, mix everything together, smooshing the avocado as you do.

Add the shredded herbs before stirring together. Season to taste. This is where you may or may not want to add the juice from the second lime – I like mine very limey. Serve right away.

Light, fresh and put together in under twenty minutes, this salad often graces my summer table. If you can get your hands on them I love to make this with a mix of yellow and green courgettes as it creates such wonderful colour. Feel free to swap out the walnuts for other nuts – with salads like this there really are no rules. This is a beautiful dish on its own but it's also lovely as a side to accompany any barbecued fish or meat on a hot summer day.

# Courgette ribbon, lemon, feta and walnut salad

**Serves 4–6**

*40–50g walnuts*

*5 medium–large courgettes (a mix of green and yellow, if you can)*

***For the dressing***

*zest of 1 ½ lemons, plus 2 tbsp juice*

*4 tbsp cold-pressed olive oil*

*1 tsp Dijon mustard*

*1 tbsp finely shredded basil (or use your favourite herb)*

*70g good-quality feta cheese*

*sea salt and black pepper*

Preheat the oven to 180°C/350°F/gas mark 4.

Arrange the walnuts on a baking tray and bake in the oven for 6–8 minutes or until they are just beginning to smell fragrant. Give them a toss halfway through. It's important not to overcook the nuts as they will continue to cook once you remove them from the oven and overcooking will give their oils a bitter taste. Leave to cool, then roughly chop.

Wash the courgettes and pat dry with kitchen paper. Then take a vegetable peeler and peel long thin slices of the courgette, working from top to bottom, and transfer the ribbons to a large bowl while you get on with the dressing.

Combine the lemon zest and juice, oil, Dijon mustard, salt and pepper in a small bowl, then drizzle the dressing over the courgettes. Add the shredded basil, about half of the crumbled feta and, using two spoons or your hands, toss the salad, making sure all the ribbons are dressed.

Just before serving, sprinkle over the toasted walnuts and crumble over the remaining feta.

Cousin to the turnip and the potato, the Jerusalem artichoke is a similar starchy root vegetable but with a much sweeter, more prominent flavour. It needs little fuss to bring out its flavour, and I find a handful of capers, some chopped dill and a simple dressing do the trick. This is delicious served hot or cold and works well alongside meat, fish or – my favourite way – with a couple of soft-boiled eggs.

# Crispy Jerusalem artichokes

*with dill and capers*

**Serves 4**

*500g Jerusalem artichokes, cut into even chunks*

*2 garlic cloves, crushed or finely chopped*

*rapeseed oil or melted butter for roasting*

*bunch of dill (about 4 tbsp), finely chopped*

*3 tbsp capers, rinsed*

*sea salt*

***For the dressing***

*2 tbsp cold-pressed olive oil*

*1 tsp wholegrain mustard*

*1 tbsp sherry vinegar or red wine vinegar*

*zest of 1 lemon, juice of ½*

Preheat the oven to 180°C/350°F/gas mark 4.

Scatter the artichokes into a roasting tin along with the garlic and drizzle with a little rapeseed oil or a knob of butter before tossing everything with a spatula to ensure the artichokes are all coated. Sprinkle with some salt and roast for about 45 minutes or until caramelised and tender.

While the artichokes are cooking, make the dressing. Mix together the olive oil, mustard, vinegar, lemon zest and juice in the bottom of your serving bowl to create a light dressing.

Add the dill and capers to the bowl and when the artichokes are done, add these too and give everything a good toss before serving.

This salad can be kept in the fridge in an airtight container for up to 4 days.

Whenever there was a picnic to attend, my mother would make her famous potato salad. The trick, she has always said, was to make it a day ahead. Inspired by the Moroccan way of eating, my own version plays on sweet and savoury with the caramel-like flavour of sweet potato paired with bold spices, garlic, crunchy toasted almonds and lavish amounts of fresh herbs. Like my mother's classic, it also tastes better when made a day ahead if possible. The recipe calls for ras el hanout, a Moroccan spice mix which is sold in many supermarkets, but if you cannot find it I have also suggested a mix of easily sourced spices that you can sub in instead.

# Moroccan sweet potato salad

**Serves 8**

*4 sweet potatoes, chopped into 2cm chunks (I prefer skin on)*

*1 tsp nigella seeds*

*1 spring onion, finely chopped*

*handful of dried apricots, roughly chopped*

*handful pitted dates, roughly chopped*

*100g flaked almonds, toasted (see page 244)*

*generous handful of coriander, roughly chopped*

*generous handful of mint, roughly chopped*

*sea salt and black pepper*

*seeds from 1 pomegranate (optional), to serve*

Steam the sweet potatoes until cooked but not too soft, about 5 minutes – you should be able to pierce them easily with a knife but they should still have some bite. Remove from the heat and leave to cool.

Meanwhile, prepare the dressing. In a pestle and mortar, roughly crush the coriander and cumin seeds. (If you don't have one, just use the end of the spice jar against the bottom of a bowl.) You don't need them to be very fine, just roughly broken. Add the garlic, oil, vinegar, spices and the orange zest. Give everything a good stir, season to taste and let it sit.

Taking your zested orange, slice off its top and tail so that you have a flat base and use a serrated knife to slice off the bitter white pith. Turn the orange on its side and loosen the segments so that you are left with just the flesh and none of the skin.

Place the cooled sweet potatoes and orange slices in a large bowl or serving dish and add the nigella seeds, spring onion, dried fruit and most of the almonds (reserving a few for sprinkling over at the end). Roughly chop the herbs and add these, too, season, then pour over the dressing and give everything a good toss with your hands. Cover, and allow the salad to rest in the fridge for a couple of hours or overnight.

*For the dressing*

*1 tsp whole coriander seeds*

*1 tsp cumin seeds*

*1 garlic clove, crushed or very finely chopped*

*6 tbsp cold-pressed olive oil*

*2 tbsp apple cider vinegar*

*1 tsp ras el hanout (or a mix of cumin, paprika, nutmeg, ground coriander and turmeric)*

*½ tsp ground turmeric*

*1 tsp mixed spice (or ground cinnamon)*

*zest of 1 orange (keep the fruit for the salad)*

*2 tbsp honey*

When you are ready to serve, sprinkle over the pomegranate seeds (if using) and a few extra almonds and chopped herbs.

This salad keeps well for up to 4 days and tastes better each day. It also travels very well.

Soft and meaty, aubergines are one of my go-to dishes when cooking vegetarian. The herby oil here not only adds a vibrant zing to this dish but also makes it look very pretty. Often I make this at parties in the run-up to Christmas, as I find the red and green colours are wonderfully festive, but it's also great cold as a delicious summer dish.

# Roasted aubergine

*with lemongrass, basil and coriander*

**Serves 4–6**

*2 aubergines, cut into 2cm sticks*

*rapeseed or olive oil, for cooking*

*1 lemongrass stalk, finely chopped*

*bunch of basil, finely chopped*

*bunch of coriander or parsley, finely chopped*

*1 garlic clove, crushed*

*zest and juice of 1 lemon*

*6 tbsp cold-pressed olive oil*

*sea salt and black pepper*

*½–1 red chilli, deseeded and finely chopped, to serve*

Preheat the oven to 180°C/350°F/gas mark 4.

Tip the aubergine sticks into a large roasting tin, drizzle with oil and massage it in with your hands. Rearrange the aubergine boats skin-side down in the tin and roast for about 25 minutes or until they are soft and browned.

Combine the lemongrass, herbs, garlic, lemon zest and juice and olive oil in a bowl and stir to make a chunky dressing – you can add as much oil and lemon juice as you like.

When the aubergines are cooked, transfer them to a serving plate and drizzle over the herby oil before sprinkling with the chilli to serve.

This is a wonderfully simple salad that is full of bold flavours. The broccoli takes on a nuttiness once roasted which marries perfectly with the wild pepperiness of the rocket and sweet tartness of the blood orange. I love this with any fish or meat dish, or even as a Sunday night supper with a few leftovers or soft-boiled eggs. If you want to eat this cold, let the broccoli and rice cool completely before mixing them with the rocket and orange – this will allow your rocket leaves to stay perky.

# Roasted broccoli, brown rice, rocket and blood orange salad

**Serves 4**

*2 blood oranges*

*1 medium head of broccoli*

*2 tbsp olive oil or coconut oil, melted*

*280g brown rice*

*200g flaked almonds, toasted (see page 244)*

*a bag of wild rocket (about 100g)*

*sea salt and black pepper*

***For the dressing***

*6 tbsp cold-pressed olive oil*

*2 tbsp apple cider vinegar*

*3 tbsp pomegranate molasses*

*1 tbsp tamari*

*1 tsp Dijon mustard*

Preheat the oven to 180°C/350°F/gas mark 4.

While the oven is warming, prepare the blood oranges. I find the easiest way is to slice the top and bottom so that you have a flat base and, using a serrated knife, work your way down the orange, removing the skin and the white pith as you go. Try to remove as much of the pith as you can. Once you have done this, turn the orange on its side and slice either side of each segment to separate them.

Remove the broccoli florets from their stalks and chop them into even-sized pieces. Trim the dry base of the stalks before slicing the rest of them into roughly 5mm slices. Transfer the broccoli to a large roasting tin and drizzle with the oil as well as a few generous grinds of salt and pepper.

Roast in the oven for about 20 minutes, tossing about halfway through, or until the broccoli is nicely charred.

Meanwhile, cook the rice according to the packet instructions. Drain.

Combine all the dressing ingredients in your serving bowl, whisking them together with a fork.

Add the broccoli, rice and three-quarters of the almonds to the bowl and toss. Add the blood orange segments and rocket and give it a light toss once more, keeping as many of the segments intact as you can. Sprinkle over the remaining almonds and serve.

I often discover a bunch of slightly floppy carrots that have been forgotten after a weekend of spontaneity, or a droopy lettuce that got lost behind the condiments. Instead of throwing these seemingly sad vegetables away I prefer to give them back some life. The great thing about this salad is that you can use whatever you have. Despite being a watery vegetable, romaine lettuce is one of my favourite things to include. Spring onions make an especially nice addition, too. You can switch and swap as you please and increase the amounts as necessary depending on how much unhappy produce you have lying about.

# Sad vegetable salad

**Serves 4–6**

*About 4 sad carrots, or any root vegetable in your fridge*

*1 head of romaine*

*2 red onions*

*1 fennel bulb*

*1 bunch of spring onions*

*3 tbsp olive oil, coconut oil or butter, plus extra for greasing*

*2 tbsp honey*

*½ tsp mixed spice*

*½ tsp ground cumin*

*thumb-sized piece of ginger, peeled and grated*

*small bunch of roughly chopped herbs (I like coriander)*

*handful of nuts or seeds, toasted (see pages 244–245)*

Preheat the oven to 200°C/400°F/gas mark 6.

Wash all the vegetables and peel any tough skin (keeping this for stock). You will probably find that the floppier the vegetable the tougher they are to peel. Don't worry, just peel as best you can. If you are using spring onions, peel off their outer tougher skin and trim off the hairy ends.

Trim the top part of the romaine and cut it into quarters. Roughly chop the vegetables into even-sized pieces and arrange all the vegetables in a large roasting tin lightly greased with oil.

In a small bowl, combine the oil or butter with the honey, mixed spice, cumin and grated ginger, stirring to combine. (Tip: use a teaspoon to peel your ginger instead of a knife. It's the best way to do it and the skin peels off incredibly easily without taking the flesh with it.) Pour this over the vegetables and roast in the oven for about 30 minutes, tossing halfway through. The roots should be cooked through and have started to char nicely.

Transfer your jewelled salad to a large serving plate and sprinkle over your herb of choice as well as a handful of toasted seeds or nuts.

My favourite way to enjoy carrots has to be roasted. Their sweetness naturally comes alive when cooked this way, and when combined with some simple kitchen cupboard spices this humble garden vegetable becomes quite exotic. I use mixed spice here as it has all the flavours I need in one, but you can use cinnamon and a pinch of nutmeg or ginger if you have it.

# Sweet carrot and hazelnut salad

*with carrot-top greens*

**Serves 4**

*about 800g organic carrots (green tops attached)*

*1 large red onion, halved and sliced into roughly 1.5cm thick pieces*

*1 garlic clove, crushed*

*rapeseed oil or coconut oil, for roasting*

*½ tsp ground turmeric*

*1 tsp mixed spice*

*1–2 tbsp honey*

*sea salt and black pepper*

*75g hazelnuts, toasted (see page 245), to serve*

Preheat the oven to 200°C/400°F/gas mark 6.

Slice the greens off the carrots and place them in a colander to wash, then leave to drain before roughly chopping. If you are using large carrots, peel them first and either slice them on the diagonal or into quarters lengthways; if you are using small ones you can leave them as they are.

Place the carrots and onion in a large roasting tin along with the garlic, oil, spices and some salt and pepper. Toss everything together using your hands and roast for 30–35 minutes or until your carrots have started to char nicely. You may want to toss them halfway through cooking.

When your carrots are close to being done, quickly heat a little coconut or rapeseed oil in a frying pan and add your carrot-top greens. Sauté them for 3–4 minutes until they have slightly wilted. Stir in the honey.

Transfer the carrots and greens to a serving plate and give everything a toss. Finish by sprinkling over the hazelnuts.

The British summer is not always known for its sunshine, and come September there are often days when I crave something a little more hearty than cold salad. Courgettes and cavolo nero come into season around June and July but they stay with us all the way until October, which makes them the perfect pair to help us with the seasonal shift from summer to autumn. Nothing can beat the comfort of a perfectly poached egg, which is the finishing touch to this warm salad. If you are not confident in your poaching abilities, fried eggs are delicious, too.

# Warm roasted courgette, cavolo nero and sunflower seed salad *with poached eggs*

**Serves 4**

*3–4 courgettes*

*1 small garlic clove, crushed or finely chopped*

*coconut oil or rapeseed oil, for roasting*

*large bunch of cavolo nero, washed*

*4 tbsp cold-pressed olive oil*

*1 tbsp apple cider vinegar*

*pinch of ground nutmeg*

*2 generous handfuls of sunflower seeds (approx 70g), toasted (see page 244)*

*1–2 eggs per person*

*sea salt and black pepper*

Preheat the oven to 200°C/400°F/gas mark 6.

Slice the courgettes on a harsh diagonal. There is no need to top and tail them and it is a common misconception that you cannot eat the stalky bit – this softens just as much as the fleshy middle, which means you get more for your courgette.

Place the courgettes in a roasting tin. Season with a little salt and pepper and sprinkle over the garlic before rubbing everything in a little rapeseed or coconut oil until coated. If your coconut oil is very solid, dot a few teaspoons around the tray and place it in the warm oven for just 5 minutes to melt. Remove the tray, toss the veg either with your hands or if the oil is too hot, a spatula, before returning to the oven. Roast for 20-25 minutes, tossing them halfway through the cooking time. They are cooked when their flesh is soft with a little char.

While the courgettes are cooking, chop the cavolo nero. I like to layer up the leaves and cut 1cm strips to create crinkly ribbons – but you can chop it however you please. Steam the cavolo nero for 3–4 minutes or until cooked but still bouncy.

Combine the olive oil, vinegar and nutmeg in a serving bowl and season to taste. Transfer the cooked cavolo nero to the bowl. Scatter over the sunflower seeds and give everything a good toss.

cont.

Now add the courgettes and toss again, going more gently this time to avoid breaking up the courgette pieces. Keep the salad warm while you poach the eggs by covering it with foil or returning it to your now switched-off oven with the door slightly ajar, as it should still have a little heat.

To poach the eggs, fill a large saucepan about one-third full of water before bringing it to the boil. Once boiling reduce the heat to a simmer.

Crack the eggs one at a time into a small bowl or ramekin and tip them into the water. Try to get them in quickly, although I don't recommend cooking more than four at a time. Cook for 3–4 minutes and remove them with a slotted spoon before draining them briefly on some kitchen paper.

If you are cooking 2 eggs per person, keep the first batch of poached eggs in a bowl of lukewarm water while you cook the second batch.

When you are ready to serve, transfer the warm salad to individual plates or a large serving bowl, carefully place the eggs on top, then sprinkle with a little black pepper and a few extra seeds.

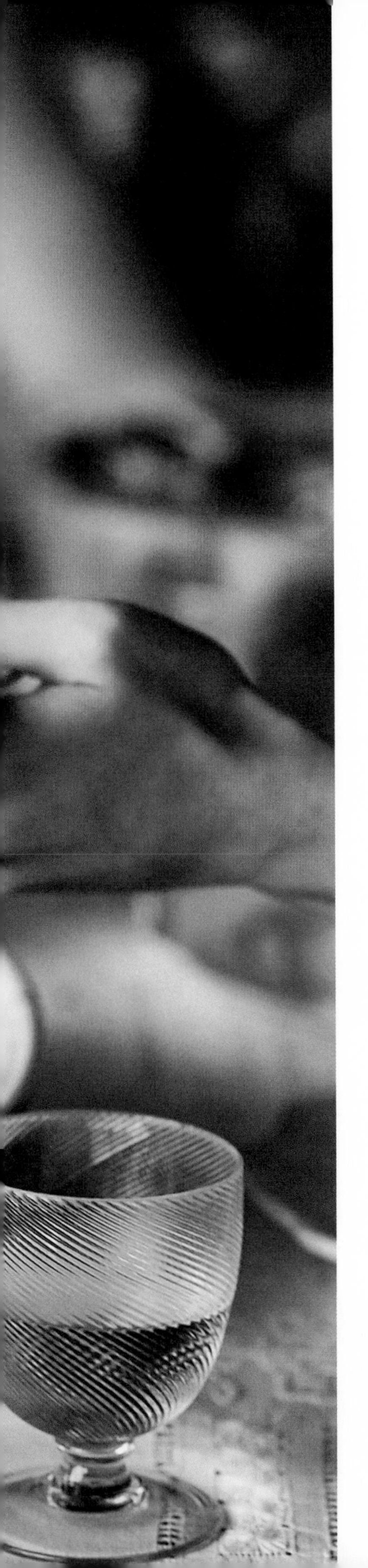

# Fish and meat

There are few things in life that are better than a home-cooked meal, and I find comfort in cooking most evenings. It winds me down and to me the preparation is often as much a joy as the final plate. Sometimes I will plan what we are eating ahead of time but often I will just see what inspires me at the fishmonger or butcher on my way home. With a few base ingredients (see pages 12–15) it needn't be overly complicated, and most of these recipes can be ready to eat in less than an hour. I eat mostly fish and white meat over red truly because I love them but my ethical consciousness plays a part too, as these options have a less-severe impact on the planet.

When choosing meat always go for organic, free-range and local if you can. When choosing fish, look for sustainably sourced ingredients – not only is it kinder to the environment but the taste is often far superior.

Sardines remind me of my mother; she eats them smashed on rye toast with a good squeeze of lemon and lots of black pepper. The smell always intrigued me as a child but it wasn't until I was older that I developed a taste for these oily little fish. Rich and slightly meaty, they are are a more sustainable fish option and tend to be incredibly good value. I'd advise you to double the chermoula recipe, as it'll keep for five days and is a great way to jazz up your meals for the next week. It also goes fantastically well with my Chargrilled herby romaine hearts (page 164), as do these sardines.

# Harissa-glazed pan-fried sardines

**Serves 4**

*with vine tomatoes and chermoula*

*2 vines of cherry tomatoes*

*1 tbsp olive oil, plus extra for greasing and drizzling*

*1 tbsp harissa paste*

*juice of ½ lemon, plus 2 lemons, halved*

*about 8 large sardines, scaled and gutted*

*sea salt and black pepper*

*toasted sourdough or rye bread, to serve*

***For the chermoula***

*bunch of coriander, roughly chopped*

*bunch of parsley leaves*

*1 garlic clove, chopped*

*zest and juice of 1 lemon*

*1 tsp ground cumin*

*½ red chilli, deseeded and roughly chopped*

*4–5 tbsp cold-pressed olive oil*

Begin by roasting the tomatoes. Preheat the oven to its highest temperature. Snip the tomato stems so that you have four separate vines, then place them on a lightly oiled baking tray and drizzle with a little more oil and add a sprinkling of sea salt. Roast in the oven for 10–12 minutes until the tops are slightly blackened and their skins are beginning to burst.

Meanwhile, start on the chermoula. Add any of the tougher herb stems to your food processor – there is no need to throw these away, just give them a little more blitz time so that you don't get any stringy bits. Next, add the remaining herbs, garlic, lemon zest and juice, cumin, chilli, some salt and pepper and the olive oil and pulse a few times to combine. It is up to you whether you go for a chunkier chermoula or a fine one. My preference changes all the time.

Next, get on with the sardines. Combine the harissa, lemon juice and 1 tablespoon of olive oil in a small bowl, then use your fingers to rub the paste over the sardines. Heat a griddle pan until hot, then cook the sardines for 2–3 minutes on each side. I like to put 4 lemon halves, flesh side down, onto the pan, too; you get a wonderfully charred look on the lemon and the heating process helps them to release their juice so they are perfect for squeezing over the sardines.

Plate up the sardines alongside the roasted cherry tomatoes and a few loose spoonfuls of the chermoula. I like to serve this with a basket of toasted sourdough or rye bread – for a smart effect you can char the toast on the hot, unoiled griddle before cooking the sardines.

I love to simply pan-fry fish with just a sprinkle of sea salt and a squeeze of lemon, but adding a bit of miso just gives it a little more of a flavour kick. It also makes for a wonderfully crispy skin, which in my eyes is the best bit. I like to use white miso for this as it has a little more sweetness. If it is a hot summer's day you can even barbecue your fish and serve the salad chilled.

# Pan-fried miso sea bass fillets

*with fennel, oranges and toasted almonds*

**Serves 4**

*4 fennel bulbs, cut into quarters*

*2 tbsp olive oil, plus extra for the fennel*

*2–3 oranges, plus extra cut into wedges*

*2 tbsp white miso paste (1 if using brown)*

*1 tbsp lemon juice*

*4 sea bass fillets (sea bream will work too)*

*knob of coconut oil or butter, for frying*

*sea salt and black pepper*

*handful of mint, finely chopped, to serve*

*handful of toasted almonds (see page 244), to serve*

Preheat the oven to 200°C/400°F/gas mark 6.

Place the fennel bulbs onto a lightly oiled roasting tray. Drizzle with olive oil, sprinkle over some salt and pepper and roast for 20–30 minutes or until they are tender and have begun to char in places.

While the fennel is cooking, prepare the oranges. I find the easiest way is to slice the top and bottom so that you have a flat base and, using a serrated knife, work your way down the orange, removing the skin and the pith as you go. Try to remove as much of the white pith as you can. Place the oranges on their sides and slice horizontally into thick discs.

Combine the miso paste, 2 tablespoons of olive oil and lemon juice in a small bowl before spreading over both sides of the fish fillets, then leave them to marinate for 15 minutes.

Heat a frying pan or griddle pan over a medium heat and melt a small knob of coconut oil or butter, just to grease the pan a little. Add the orange slices and cook for about 3 minutes either side or until they have caramelised slightly and have begun to smell fragrant. Transfer them to a plate, keeping any remaining juices in the pan. Make sure the pan is not too hot or the sweetness of the miso will cause the fish to burn. Place the fillets skin side down and cook for about 2 minutes before flipping over. Cook the second side for a further 1–2 minutes or until the fish is completely cooked through and opaque. (If your pan cannot hold all four at one time, cook them in batches and keep the cooked fillets on a warm plate covered with parchment or foil.)

Arrange the fennel and oranges onto the plates, squeezing over any excess juice from the skins or chopping board. Sprinkle over the mint and almonds and place the cooked fish on top. Serve with a wedge of orange.

One of my favourite shops is called the Fish Shed: a little shack on the side of the road, it is about a ten-minute stroll from my family home in Norfolk. Everything is always incredibly fresh and they even smoke their own fish in a small shed on site. This mackerel recipe is wonderfully simple. If you ask your fishmonger to gut and scale the fish for you, most of your work is done. The green rice is equally easy to prepare and can be enjoyed hot or cold. I've suggested my favourite herbs here, but feel free to switch them around as you prefer. I like to make a fresh mayonnaise to go with this, such as the one on page 181, but you can also enjoy it just as it is.

# Smoked paprika mackerel

*with zesty herby rice*

**Serves 4**

*4 whole mackerel, scaled and gutted (or filleted)*

*sea salt and black pepper*

**For the marinade**

*1 tbsp smoked paprika*

*½ tsp cayenne pepper*

*3 tbsp olive oil*

*1 garlic clove, crushed*

*1 tsp tamari*

**For the zesty herby rice**

*200g brown rice*

*bunch of basil, leaves and stems separated*

*bunch of coriander, leaves and stems separated*

*1 garlic clove, crushed*

*zest of 2 lemons, juice of 1, 1 cut into wedges*

*6 tbsp cold-pressed olive oil, plus extra to serve*

First, prepare your fish by scoring it on the diagonal, giving it three slashes on each side.

Next, combine all the marinade ingredients in a bowl. Rub this onto the outside and inside of the fish, making sure you get right into the cavity. If you are using fillets, simply rub the marinade over each side. Allow to marinate for about 10 minutes.

Meanwhile, cook the rice according to the packet instructions.

When the fish has marinated, heat a frying pan or griddle pan to a medium–high heat and add the mackerel (you may need to do this in two stages; put the first two cooked fish on a plate and cover in foil to keep warm while you cook the others. Cook for 3–4 minutes on each side or until cooked through and charred.

For the zesty herby rice, roughly chop the stems of both herbs and transfer them to a food processor along with the garlic, lemon zest and juice, olive oil, salt and pepper. Pulse until it is beginning to take on a pesto appearance. At this point add about three-quarters of the herb leaves and give it all a few more pulses to combine. I like to have a variety of herb texture in the rice. I love using my mini Magimix for this but if you don't have a food processor you can simply do this by hand, or use a pestle and mortar to create more of a sauce-like texture.

Drain the cooked rice, then pour in the zesty green mix as well as a little more olive oil and salt and pepper, if needed, then stir to combine. Divide among individual plates with the mackerel alongside or transfer to one large serving bowl. Serve sprinkled with the remaining herbs and wedges of lemon.

I love the richness of this soup. It reminds me of long summer lunches that roll into evenings. It also makes the house smell wonderful and hence I love to make it when I am entertaining. You can serve it as a starter or as a main. I tend to go with the latter and fill the table with informal and oversized baskets of various breads. If I get time I make my croutons in advance and store them in an airtight container. They are brilliant for tossing into salads or crunching on with a glass of something cold.

# Provençal seafood soup

*with baked polenta croutons*

**Serves 4**

***For the croutons***
*(makes 50–60)*

*3 tbsp olive oil, plus extra for crisping the croutons*

*good pinch of salt*

*80g polenta (cornmeal), fine or coarse*

***For the soup***

*4 tbsp olive oil*

*1 leek, finely sliced*

*60g cured black olives, roughly chopped*

*1 tbsp capers, roughly chopped*

*1 garlic clove, crushed or finely chopped*

*2 tbsp tomato purée*

*2 handfuls of spinach leaves*

*400g tin organic, no-added-salt chopped tomatoes*

*250ml vegetable or fish stock*

*75ml dry white wine (or more stock)*

First make the croutons. Line a rectangular baking tin with cling film – I use one that's 20 x 20cm.

Bring 450ml of water to the boil in a large saucepan and stir in the oil and salt. Gradually pour in the polenta, whisking constantly as you do. Reduce the heat to low and continue to whisk for about 5 minutes or until it has thickened and is slightly pulling away from the sides. Pour it into the lined tin and smooth the top with an oiled spatula. Work quickly as the polenta will begin to cool and harden as soon as it is off the heat. Leave to sit at room temperature for about 15 minutes, then cover it in cling film and transfer it to the fridge for half an hour to set fully.

Once set, turn out the polenta onto a clean surface and remove the cling film. Cut the polenta into roughly 1cm squares. You can also make them larger if you prefer.

Preheat the oven to 240°C/475°F/gas mark 9. While it is heating up, pour some olive oil into a small bowl and one by one brush the sides of your polenta squares with oil using a pastry brush before placing them on a baking tray. Bake in the oven for 30–40 minutes or until crispy, turning them over about halfway through the cooking time. If you are making larger croutons you may need to cook them a little longer, as you want them to be nice and crisp.

Meanwhile, make the soup. Add the olive oil and leek to a large pan and heat gently to soften. You may want to add a tablespoon or so of water to prevent the leek from browning. Once soft, add the olives, capers, garlic and tomato purée and stir for a few minutes to combine. Stir in the spinach and cook until most of the leaves have wilted down.

*1 medium fennel bulb, cut into 5mm slices*

*100g squid, chopped into rings*

*120g prawns, shelled*

*150g firm white fish (such as cod or haddock), chopped into roughly 4cm chunks*

*bunch of parsley or basil, roughly chopped*

Pour in the tin of tomatoes, stock, white wine, if using, or more stock, and fennel and heat until the mixture is gently simmering. Add the squid and prawns, then give the mix a quick stir before placing the white fish on top. Cover with a lid and cook for about 3 minutes or until the fish is cooked through and the flesh is opaque.

Season to taste and serve with a sprinkle of chopped herbs and a handful of polenta croutons.

Incredibly easy to throw together, poke is one of those dishes that I make when I don't feel like spending hours in the kitchen but still want to make something spectacular. A traditional Hawaiian dish, poke came to be when the fishermen began making use of the offcuts from their catch, seasoning them to eat as a snack. Bright, colourful and zingy, it is a dish I love serving to friends in the summer – it has a wonderfully exotic feel to it, despite being quite effortless to prepare. I tend to make this with salmon rather than tuna as it is usually the more sustainable option. Be sure to use sushi-grade salmon – any good fishmonger should be able to help.

# Salmon poke bowl

*with coconut black rice*

**Serves 4**

*about 500g sushi-grade salmon*

*½ red onion, finely sliced*

*2 spring onions, finely chopped*

*4 tbsp tamari (gluten-free soy sauce)*

*1 tbsp sesame oil*

*2 tbsp rice wine vinegar or apple cider vinegar*

*thumb-sized piece of ginger, peeled and grated*

*1 avocado, peeled, stoned and cut into cubes*

*2 tbsp sesame seeds – black, white or a mix*

**For the rice**

*200g black risotto or sushi rice*

*400ml tin full-fat coconut milk*

*pinch of salt*

***To garnish (optional)***

*grated radish*

*grated carrot*

*fresh sliced chilli*

*pickled ginger*

Begin by cooking the rice, as you will want this to be cold by the time you are ready to serve.

Put the rice in a large saucepan with a pinch of salt and the coconut milk and then using the coconut milk can to pour in about half a can's worth of water. This is also a great way to ensure you get all of the coconut milk out of the can, so none goes to waste. Bring the liquid to the boil, giving it a stir to ensure all the creamy coconut has infused into the water. Once the liquid is bubbling, reduce the heat to a simmer and leave for about 30 minutes. Check after 15, adding more water if needed.

Once the rice is cooked, remove it from the heat and allow it to cool. Prepare the salmon, beginning by removing any bones before chopping it into 1cm cubes. Set aside.

In a medium bowl, combine the sliced onion, spring onions, tamari, sesame oil, vinegar and ginger. Give it a stir before adding the salmon and using either a spoon or your hands to coat the salmon with the marinade. Place the salmon in the fridge to marinate and chill for at least an hour.

When it is time to serve, remove the salmon from the fridge and add the avocado and sesame seeds, stirring gently to combine. Plate up your rice, then top with the salmon poke and garnish with grated radish, carrots, chilli and pickled ginger, if you like.

Ceviche is a wonderfully fresh dish that originates from Latin America, mainly Peru, and is made by curing fresh raw fish in citrus juices. Unlike sushi, it is heavily flavoured with spices such as chilli and lots of herbs. I love using British strawberries here to give this dish a bit of a local slant; I generally use mint from the garden, but coriander is also delicious. If you can't get hold of sea bass you could use cod. I love to serve this on a big sharing platter for people to fill their plates from, alongside a few simple salads (see pages 178–180).

# Sea bass and strawberry ceviche

*with broad bean and mint*

**Serves 4**

*500g sea bass, scaled with skin on or off, filleted and pinboned (this means removing the very fine bones. You can ask your fishmonger to do this)*

*zest of 1 lime and juice of 3*

*½ red chilli, deseeded and finely chopped*

*150g strawberries*

*about 15 pods of broad beans, shelled, blanched and cooled*

*cold-pressed extra-virgin olive oil, for drizzling*

*small bunch of mint leaves, to serve*

*sea salt and black pepper*

Using a sharp knife, cut the fish into thin slices roughly 5mm thick. Place the fish in a large bowl and keep it cool in the fridge while you prepare the rest of the ingredients.

In a small bowl mix the lime zest and juice, chilli and 1 teaspoon of sea salt and set aside in the fridge.

When you are ready to serve, finely slice the strawberries and transfer them to the bowl with the fish, along with the broad beans. Pour over the dressing and lightly toss with your hands to coat, taking care not to break up too many of the strawberries.

Let the ceviche rest for about 5 minutes then transfer either to a large platter or individual plates. Drizzle with a little olive oil, scatter with fresh mint and finish with a good grind of black pepper. Eat straight away.

For years I believed that the 'black' part of 'black cod' was simply a reference to the way it was cooked. It was only when I spent an evening with a fantastic Japanese chef that I learned that usually what we are eating when we eat 'black cod' is sablefish or butterfish. It has a much higher fat content than regular cod and hence usually comes at a higher price. So for this dish I use halibut – an equally delicious white fish which is slightly more affordable, but you could use regular cod too. The recipe calls for a few traditional ingredients that are used in Japanese cooking. If you can't get these, I have suggested a few substitutes instead.

# Quick miso 'black' halibut

*with candied leeks*

**Serves 4**

***For the halibut***

*2 heaped tbsp brown rice miso paste*

*1 tbsp Japanese rice wine vinegar (or use apple cider vinegar)*

*2 tbsp toasted sesame oil*

*2 tbsp mirin (or add an extra tablespoon each of vinegar and honey)*

*2 tbsp honey*

*4 good-sized halibut or cod fillets (skin on)*

***For the candied leeks***

*4 leeks, washed and trimmed*

*1 tbsp brown rice miso paste*

*1 tbsp toasted sesame oil*

Preheat the oven to 200°C/400°F/gas mark 6.

In a small mixing bowl, combine the miso paste, rice wine vinegar, sesame oil, mirin and honey.

Line a baking tray with foil or baking parchment. Place the fish fillets on the tray and cover them with the marinade, turning to coat them. Place the fish skin side up and leave to marinate whilst preparing the leeks.

Cut the leeks into three, halve each chunk lengthways then cut these into thinner strips or juliennes. There is no need to be too precious here.

Combine the miso paste, sesame oil and mirin in a small bowl.

Heat the oil in a frying pan over a medium heat, add the leeks and cook until softened. If you find the leeks are browning too much, reduce the heat and add a couple of tablespoons of water.

Add the miso mix to the leeks and stir through. Remove from the heat and loosely cover the pan with a lid to keep warm while you cook the fish.

*1 tbsp mirin (or use the substitute suggested above)*

*3 tbsp coconut oil or rapeseed oil*

*toasted sesame seeds, for sprinkling (optional)*

Place the baking tray of halibut onto a rack in the top half of the oven and cook the fish for 12 minutes, but keep an eye on it. I like to switch my oven setting to the grill for the final 3 minutes of cooking time, just to give the skin a little bit of crisp, but it isn't essential. You could also use this time to give your leeks another quick session on the heat. They should be soft, sticky and golden by now.

Check to see that the fish is cooked through – the flesh should be opaque. Plate up the leeks and fish fillets, drizzling over any of the cooking juices in the tray, and sprinkle with the sesame seeds to serve.

The smell of this always reminds me of when I spent a summer working in an Italian restaurant. They would make huge vats of the most incredible tomato and oregano sauce which would be used as a base for pasta, pizza and vegetable dishes. The combination of tomato and oregano is flawless and transforms simple white fish into a rich, flavourful dish. I like to use smoked cod for this as I rather enjoy its smokiness against the sweet tomatoes, but unsmoked fish is also delicious.

# Tomato, oregano and basil warming fish bake

**Serves 4–6**

***You will need a large deep roasting tray***

*2 large or 3 medium-sized courgettes, cut into 2cm rounds or pieces*

*1 large red onion, quartered*

*olive oil, for drizzling*

*about 900g boneless firm white fish, smoked or unsmoked (halibut, cod, haddock, hake), cut into (4-8) even sized pieces*

*2 garlic cloves, crushed or finely chopped*

*2 x 400g tins organic, no-added-salt chopped tomatoes*

*1 tbsp balsamic vinegar*

*100g pitted black olives*

*1 tbsp dried oregano or rosemary*

*2 tbsp roughly chopped fresh oregano leaves, plus extra sprigs*

Preheat the oven to 180°C/350°F/gas mark 4.

Place the courgettes and onion in a large, deep roasting tray and drizzle with olive oil. Bake for about 30 minutes or until slightly browned.

Add the garlic, tinned tomatoes, balsamic vinegar, olives, dried herbs, fresh oregano and a good pinch each of salt and pepper. Give everything a good stir to make a thick, chunky sauce.

Arrange the fish, cherry tomato vines and any remaining oregano sprigs on top of the sauce and bake in the oven for 15–18 minutes or until your fish has cooked through.

Remove from the oven and tear over the basil leaves while the fish is still hot, allowing them to wilt slightly.

Serve warm from the oven with rice, potatoes or my White miso cauliflower mash (see page 167) and a big green salad.

*1–2 bunches of cherry tomatoes on the vine, cut into 4 stalks*

*bunch of basil leaves*

*sea salt and black pepper*

The trick to cooking squid is all in the timing; just three seconds too long and it can turn from buttery soft to rubber ring. For the perfect bite, watch your squid like a hawk – as soon as it turns white, take it off the heat. I am a little bit of a sauce fiend and the romano jam is a delicious addition here, especially if you are serving the squid with some rice or potatoes that need a bit of perking up.

# Spicy grilled squid

*with balsamic romano jam*

**Serves 4**

*about 450g whole squid (with tentacles), cleaned*

*2 tsp dry harissa spice mix or smoked paprika*

*½ tsp cayenne pepper*

*½ tsp ground cumin*

*1 garlic clove, crushed*

*1 lemon*

*4 tbsp extra virgin olive oil*

*sea salt and freshly ground black pepper*

***For the balsamic romano jam***

*4 romano peppers*

*olive oil, for roasting*

*1 tbsp balsamic vinegar*

*fresh lemon juice (optional), to squeeze over*

*sea salt and black pepper*

*wooden skewers if using baby squid*

Preheat the oven to 200°C/400°F/gas mark 6.

Begin by making your quick romano jam. Place the peppers, with their stems still on, onto a large baking tray. Rub them all over with olive oil and roast in the oven for about 30 minutes until they are soft and slightly charred. Remove from the oven and allow them to cool slightly.

Once cool, using a sharp knife score a small slit at the top of the pepper right below the stalk. Gently pluck off the stalks and they should take with them the seedy core. If there are a few seeds left, remove as many as you can with a spoon.

Transfer the peppers to a small bowl and, using just a table knife and fork, roughly chop them. Add the balsamic vinegar, a little salt and pepper and, using your fork again, give the peppers a vigorous whisk. They should break down very easily, leaving you with a textured, jam-like sauce. Set aside. If you like a little more tang you could add some more vinegar or fresh lemon juice.

If the squid are large, begin by scoring one side of their bodies. They will be tender so be careful not to cut all the way through to the other side and break the body. A trick is to gently place a large chopping knife in the cavity of the squid before scoring to prevent your knife from chopping all the way through. If your squids are baby ones, soak wooden skewers in a bowl of cold water while the squid is marinating and thread the squids onto them just before cooking. Once prepared, place the squid into a bowl just big enough to hold them.

In a small bowl, mix the harissa or paprika with the cayenne pepper, cumin, garlic, the zest of the lemon, olive oil and some salt and pepper until you have a paste. Use your hands to coat the squid with the marinade, then leave it to marinate for about 15 minutes.

Heat the bbq grill or a griddle pan and when hot, place the squid on the hottest part of the grill. Cook for 2–3 minutes, tossing them every thirty seconds. Remove the squid as soon as they turn opaque.

Plate up the squid and serve with fresh lemon wedges and a spoonful of the romano jam.

I love making this as an easy weekday supper dish. Usually I will serve it with some simple brown rice flavoured with just the zest of a lemon and some good olive oil, as the yoghurty marinade acts adds a wonderful 'self-saucing' element to the dish. I like to quickly peel a courgette into ribbons and bung it in the pan with a little oil and garlic for a minute or so, but any green works well. The whole thing can be made start to finish in 30 minutes, and I always go to bed feeling well nourished and well fed after eating this.

## Zingy turmeric, coconut yoghurt and basil grilled cod

**Serves 2**

*2 skinless cod fillets (about 175g each)*

*sea salt and black pepper*

***For the marinade***

*6 tbsp coconut yoghurt (you could also use Greek yoghurt)*

*1 lemongrass stalk, finely chopped*

*1 garlic clove, crushed or finely chopped*

*½ tsp ground turmeric*

*small bunch of basil, finely shredded, plus extra for garnishing*

***To serve***

*cooked brown rice*

*wokked or steamed greens, courgette, mangetout or green beans*

Combine the yoghurt, lemongrass, garlic, turmeric and basil in a bowl or a medium ovenproof dish. (I like to create as little washing up as possible so tend to do everything in the serving dish if I can!) Once the yoghurt has taken on a good golden colour and the basil and garlic have been evenly incorporated, coat the fish fillets in the mix and leave to marinate for 20 minutes.

Preheat the grill to high and grill the fish for about 4 minutes on each side or until cooked through.

Serve with brown rice and some simple steamed greens or flash-fried vegetables, then spoon over any leftover yoghurty cooking juices and sprinkle with some fresh basil.

I am one of those people who doesn't hold back when eating whole fish on the bone; I will pull off every last buttery morsel to leave a clean skeleton on my plate. This fish is no exception, the skin being even more delicious paired with puddles of salty, sticky olives. For this reason I tend to serve this alongside small bowls of lemon-infused water to cleanse fishy fingers in between bites.

# Rosemary bream

*with roasted romanesco, lemon and battered black olives*

**Serves 2**

*olive or rapeseed oil, for greasing*

*2 whole bream fish, scaled and gutted*

*2 garlic cloves, finely sliced*

*handful of rosemary leaves, roughly chopped*

*2 lemons, finely sliced, and juice of ½ lemon*

*1 head of romanesco cauliflower*

*1 tbsp olive oil*

*4 tbsp white wine or water*

*about 70g dry-cured, pitted black olives (or Kalamata)*

*sea salt and black pepper*

*lemon slices and lemon water, to serve*

Preheat the oven to 200°C/400°F/gas mark 6 and grease a very large roasting tray which will fit the fish and all the other ingredients with oil.

Slice each side of the fish on the diagonal to create three slits, then rub them with a little olive oil and stuff the slits and cavity with garlic, rosemary and the slices from one lemon. Set aside.

Chop the romanesco florets into roughly 2cm-sized pieces and the stalk into 1cm chunks, then transfer to the roasting tray. Arrange the remaining lemon slices evenly among the romanesco. Drizzle over the olive oil, lemon juice and sprinkle with a good pinch of salt.

Place into the oven for 10–15 minutes, then momentarily pull the tray out of the oven, push the romanesco to the side and place the two fish in the centre. Try to leave a little space between them so that they are not touching, as they will cook better this way.

Pour over the wine or water and leave to cook for a further 20 minutes until the romanesco is charred and the fish is cooked through.

While the fish is cooking, prepare the olives. Roll out about an A4-size piece of cling film and place the olives about halfway up, folding over the bottom part of the cling film to cover them, almost creating a little envelope. Using either a rolling pin or the back of a wooden spoon, give them a good beating until they are roughly broken down and battered. Transfer to a small bowl and set aside.

Divide the romanesco and fish evenly between your plates and dot over spoonfuls of the battered olives. Serve each plate with a slice of fresh lemon and bowls of the lemon water.

For a very long time I believed that I didn't like risotto. Whenever I had eaten it at restaurants I had found it too heavy and too rich, and was bored after the first few mouthfuls. It was my boyfriend's mother who turned around my distaste for the dish. The first time I went to visit his family home she cooked chicken risotto and it was utterly delicious. Made with homemade chicken stock and just a little Parmesan, it was so much lighter than what I'd been used to. Since then I have played around with making my own. For an entirely vegetarian version of this dish, swap the scallops for some asparagus, chop the spears into chunks and pan-fry them until slightly charred.

# Zesty lemon, pea and scallop risotto

**Serves 4–6**

*500g peas, cooked and cooled*

*1.5 litres chicken, fish or vegetable stock*

*8 tbsp butter or coconut oil, plus a knob for frying*

*3 shallots, finely chopped*

*400g Arborio rice*

*200ml dry white wine (for an alcohol-free version just use water or more stock, although the alcohol content is mostly eliminated during cooking)*

*zest of 1 lemon, keep the lemon to serve as wedges*

*50g Parmesan (optional)*

*400g scallops, cleaned*

*small bunch of mint*

*sea salt and black pepper*

Place about half the peas and about 100ml of the chicken stock in a blender or food processor and blend until smooth. Set aside.

In a medium pan, heat the remaining stock so that it is warm but not boiling.

Place a large deep frying pan over a medium heat and add 4 tablespoons of the butter or coconut oil and the shallots. Cook, stirring, until soft – about 5 minutes.

Stir in the rice and add the wine, if using. Let it cook until most of the liquid has evaporated. At this point add a ladle or two of stock. Stir gently and add more stock once all the liquid has nearly gone. Repeat for about 15 minutes, then check to see whether the rice is cooked – it should be slightly glutinous but still have bite. If it is not done, continue to add the stock until the rice has reached the ideal consistency, leaving 1 tablespoon for the peas.

Season with salt and pepper and stir in 2 tablespoons of butter or coconut oil, the lemon zest and Parmesan, if using.

Fold in the pea purée and the remaining whole peas. Season to taste, add just a tablespoon more stock and leave off the heat, but covered, while you sear the scallops.

Ensure the scallops are very dry by patting them with some kitchen paper. They will crisp up nicely this way. Melt a knob of butter or coconut oil in a non-stick pan. Season both sides of the scallops with salt and a little pepper before adding them to the hot pan. They will cook better if they are not touching, so use a large pan or cook in batches. Cook for about 8 minutes, turning halfway through the time. They should have taken on some nice colour but still be soft.

Taste the risotto and add more seasoning or liquid if needed. Spoon into bowls and divide the scallops among them equally. Tear over some mint leaves and serve with a wedge of lemon to squeeze over and grated parmesan, if you like. Serve straight away.

I still reminisce about the tagines I ate during a trip to Marrakesh; the one I remember most was eaten way up in the Atlas Mountains, at the home of a cherry farmer. The tagine was sweet but spiced, studded with the softest of dates and tart cherries. In my own version, the broken cauliflower adds a bit more crunch to the dish whilst doing a wonderful job of soaking up the beautifully fragrant sauce from the chicken. If you are making this outside of cherry season, pomegranate seeds also work very well.

# Slow-cooked Moroccan chicken

*with broken cauliflower and cherries*

**Serves 4–6**

*2 knobs of coconut oil or butter*

*1 medium chicken, separated into 10 pieces (or 8–10 chicken thighs)*

*2 red onions, finely sliced*

*2 garlic cloves, crushed*

*thumb-sized piece of ginger, peeled and finely chopped*

*½ tsp ground turmeric*

*1 tsp ground cinnamon*

*1 pinch of saffron*

*2 tsp ras el hanout (Moroccan spice blend, or use mixed spice)*

*1 tsp ground coriander*

*1 tsp ground cumin*

*2 large carrots, peeled and cut on the diagonal*

*1 preserved lemon, sliced (or use ½ a fresh one)*

*300ml chicken or vegetable stock*

Begin by melting the coconut oil or butter in a large heavy-based saucepan, then fry the chicken in batches until browned. At this point it does not need to be cooked right through. Remove the chicken from the pan and set aside.

Add the onions, garlic and ginger and fry for about 4 minutes or until softened. If the onions are browning too quickly, add a few tablespoons of water. Next, stir in the spices before returning the chicken to the pan and coating it in the spice mix.

Add the carrots, lemon and stock and bring to the boil, then reduce the heat to a simmer, cover with a lid and cook for about 45 minutes.

Remove the lid and stir in the dates. Cook for another 35–45 minutes with the lid off until the chicken is tender.

While the chicken is cooking, prepare the cauliflower. Begin by placing the stalks in the food processor and pulsing until they are almost rice-like. Transfer to a bowl. Repeat this process with the florets, breaking them down in batches. It's quite nice to keep some of the cauliflower pieces larger than others.

Once all your cauliflower has been broken down, melt the coconut oil or butter in a second large saucepan or deep frying pan and add the spices, a good pinch of salt and just a couple of splashes of water. Tip in the cauliflower and toss it in the spice mix until it has taken on a good yellow colour. Continue to stir it while it cooks, adding about 100ml of water bit by bit, as you would for a risotto, until the cauliflower is cooked – you may like to add a little more water, but not too much as the water should all be absorbed in the cooking process. After about 10

*handful of dates, stones removed*

*sea salt and black pepper*

*2 tbsp chopped fresh parsley or coriander, to serve*

**For the broken cauliflower**

*2–3 heads of cauliflower, florets separated and stalks cut into roughly 1-inch sized pieces*

*knob of coconut oil or butter*

*1 tsp ground turmeric*

*½ tsp ground coriander*

*pinch of cayenne pepper*

*4 tbsp cold-pressed, extra-virgin olive oil*

*2 tbsp chopped fresh parsley or coriander*

*2 tbsp chopped fresh mint*

*200g flaked almonds, toasted (see page 244)*

*70g chopped pistachios*

*1 punnet of cherries, stones removed and halved (or the seeds of 2 pomegranate fruits)*

minutes, test the cauliflower; when you pierce it with the point of a knife it should be cooked all the way through but still have a little bite. Season to taste then drizzle over the olive oil and stir through the herbs and cherries (or pomegranate seeds) and nuts, keeping a handful or so aside for last-minute garnishing.

Check the chicken – the sauce should have thickened slightly by now – and season to taste.

Divide the broken cauliflower between bowls and ladle over the chicken, making sure everyone gets a good amount of sauce. Finish with a sprinkle of herbs and almonds, if you like, and serve.

My mother was brought up in Africa and she was always able to hypnotise my siblings and me with her stories. These ranged from her climbing banana trees to having pet monkeys steal her mother's cupcakes. Something else that kept us well behaved was when she would make her jungle curry. The best bit was the toppings, which my mother said was what made the curry a jungle one. She would put out little bowls of freshly chopped banana, oranges, papaya and coconut as well as hot-out-of-the-oven toasted peanuts and raisins that we would pile over our plates. It still tastes best when she makes it – perhaps there is another secret. But this recipe is quite delicious and rather fun for when you have friends round.

# My mother's jungle curry

**Serves 4–6**

*2 knobs of coconut oil*

*2 red onions, roughly chopped*

*8–10 skinless chicken thighs on the bone*

*400ml tin full-fat coconut milk*

*400g tin organic chopped tomatoes*

*1 sweet potato, peeled and cut into cubes*

*4 whole green chillies*

*about 80g rice per person*

*zest and juice of 1 lemon*

*sea salt and black pepper*

***For the paste***

*1 tbsp ground turmeric*

*1 tsp garam masala*

*2 tsp whole coriander seeds*

*1 tsp ground cumin*

*1 tsp cayenne pepper*

Begin by making the curry paste. Toast all the spices in a dry pan over a medium heat for a few minutes or until they begin to smell fragrant. Transfer the spices to a food processor along with the rest of the paste ingredients and whizz to a paste.

Now start on the curry. Melt 1 knob of coconut oil in a large pan, then add the onions and cook until softened. If they are browning too quickly, add a little water. Stir in the curry paste, add the chicken and cook until browned, turning the pieces over to coat them well.

Pour in the coconut milk, tomatoes, sweet potato and whole green chillies. Bring to the boil before reducing the heat to a simmer, then cook for 45 minutes–1 hour, stirring occasionally and allowing the liquid to reduce slightly.

Meanwhile, cook the rice according to the packet instructions. Drain, then stir the lemon zest and the remaining coconut oil through the rice and season to taste.

Fish out the chillies from the curry, season to taste and check that the chicken is cooked through – it should pull away easily from the bone. If you like you can remove the bones and shred the meat slightly using two forks.

Make sure all the topping ingredients are ready chopped and placed in little bowls around the table, then serve up the rice and curry in big bowls, letting everyone serve themselves and choose the toppings for their own curry.

*thumb-sized piece of ginger, peeled and finely chopped*

*2 garlic cloves, finely chopped*

*1 fresh green or red chilli*

*2 tbsp organic, no-added-sugar tomato purée*

**For topping**

*bunch of coriander, roughly chopped*

*peeled and chopped oranges*

*peeled and chopped bananas*

*freshly shaved coconut and desiccated coconut*

*peeled and chopped papaya*

*plain roasted peanuts*

*sultanas or raisins*

This curry should keep for up to 4 days in the fridge and you can enjoy the leftovers reheated gently over the hob for about 20 minutes or until piping hot. I'd advise cooking fresh rice if it is any older than 1 day old (old rice can often give one a stomach upset). If you are reheating your rice be sure to make it piping hot before consuming.

Another way to enjoy the leftover curry is to add a couple of spoonful's of Greek or coconut yoghurt. This makes for a bit of a cheats coronation chicken and is a delicious cold lunch contender.

I first made this one Sunday in April when the weather was, by English standards, prematurely hot. The prospect of roast potatoes and gravy seemed all too wintery, so I was left with the challenge of turning our Sunday roast into something a little lighter. We swapped our buttered cabbage for a cool cucumber salad and scattered the whole thing with mint from the garden. This chicken is rich with flavour and the addition of peanut butter also keeps the meat wonderfully tender. Most butchers will spatchcock the chicken for you if you ask them, but if you are working with a whole bird, see my tip below on how to do this yourself.

# Spatchcocked Persian-spiced peanut butter chicken *with pinked onion, cucumber and pomegranate slaw*

**Serves 4–6**

*1 chicken (about 1.3kg), whole (see tip) or spatchcocked*

*1 tsp turmeric*

*2 tsp mixed spice*

*1 tsp sumac*

*1 heaped tbsp peanut butter*

*2 tbsp olive oil*

*1 tbsp apple cider vinegar*

*sea salt and black pepper*

*crusty loaf, to serve*

***For the slaw***

*1 red onion, finely sliced*

*5 tbsp red wine vinegar*

*4 limes*

*3 tbsp cold-pressed olive oil*

*1 cucumber*

*seeds of 1 pomegranate*

*bunch of mint leaves, finely chopped*

First prepare the chicken. If it is a whole chicken, spatchcock the bird. To do this, you'll need some good, sharp kitchen scissors. On a flat surface, place your chicken breast side down (which will look like upside down to the usual roasting way).

Working from the thigh end, cut all the way along one side of the backbone. Rotate the chicken and cut down the other side in the same way, releasing the backbone as you do (you can keep this for stock). Flip the chicken over and transfer to a roasting tray.

Next, combine the turmeric, mixed spice, sumac, peanut butter, oil and vinegar in a small bowl. Season well, then rub the mix all over the bird. Try to work some of the marinade under the skin if you can – I usually find there is one side where the skin seems to give more easily, but with a little pushing you normally have luck. Cover, put in the fridge and leave the chicken to marinate for 2–4 hours while you prepare the slaw.

Place the onion in a small bowl and add the red wine vinegar and the juice from three of the limes. Cover with cling film and leave to steep in the fridge for at least 2 hours. You'll notice the onions turn a bright pink as they start to slightly pickle.

cont.

Take 2 tablespoons of the steeping juice from your onions and place it in a serving bowl along with the olive oil and the juice of half of the remaining lime. Mix and season to taste. You may want to add the rest of your lime juice. Drain and rinse the onions before adding them to the bowl.

Slice the cucumber in half lengthways and scoop out the seedy centre using a teaspoon. Cut the cucumber halves on the diagonal into thin slices and add these to the onions. Toss everything together and keep cool until ready to serve.

Preheat the barbecue until the coals are white hot, or if you are using an oven, preheat it to 200°C/400°F/gas mark 6. The cooking time for the chicken is dependent on the method you use as well as your specific oven or barbecue, but as a rough guideline I recommend 40–50 minutes in the oven or 35–40 on the barbecue. Check the chicken is cooked through – if you pierce the thigh of the chicken the juices should run clear but the meat should be deliciously tender. If any there is any pink in the juice, leave the chicken to cook for a little longer.

When you are just about ready to serve, throw the chopped mint leaves and pomegranate seeds into your slaw and give everything a toss. Transfer the chicken to a serving dish and roughly divide it into legs, breasts and wings, letting everyone pick and choose their favourite cut. Any leftover juices in the serving dish will be delicious, so serve slices of a good crusty loaf for mopping them up.

Sunflower seeds create the perfect crust here, and although primarily made of seeds the topping is rich and nutty with a bounce of chilli running through. I tend to serve this with couple of quick and colourful salads (see pages 178–180).

# Toasted sunflower seed, chilli and lemongrass crusted salmon

**Serves 4**

*4 tbsp sunflower seeds*

*2 tbsp olive oil, plus extra for drizzling*

*4 salmon fillets (with or without skin)*

*2 lemongrass stalk, finely chopped*

*½ red or green chilli, finely chopped*

*just larger than a thumb-sized piece of ginger, peeled and grated*

*2 tsp apple cider vinegar*

*sea salt and black pepper*

*lime wedges, to serve*

Begin by toasting the sunflower seeds in a dry frying pan over a medium–high heat. Toast for 8–10 minutes or until they are lightly browned and release a fragrant, nutty smell. Transfer to a plate to cool.

Preheat the oven to 200°C/400°F/gas mark 6 and line a medium baking tray with tin foil. Drizzle a little olive oil over the tray to grease it slightly and add the fillets (skin-side down if they have skin).

Once the sunflower seeds have cooled, chop them into roughly 2–3mm-sized pieces. Combine the seeds, lemongrass, chilli, ginger, 2 tablespoons of olive oil, vinegar, salt and pepper in a bowl, then spread the mix over the salmon fillets. Bake for 10–12 minutes or until the salmon is cooked through.

Serve the fish with lime wedges on the side.

I love to cook these in the summer for a lighter twist on the burger and sausage barbecue line-up. They are delicious with the tabbouleh salad, but you can serve them with any salad or salads that you wish – usually I will make at least one or two sharing salads (pages 178–180). You can cook the koftas on the barbecue on a lovely summer's day, or under the grill on a not-so-lovely summer's day!

# Turkey and apricot koftas

*with buckwheat tabbouleh salad and sweet tahini dressing*

**Serves 4**

***For the tabbouleh***

*200g toasted buckwheat groats*

*bunch of fresh mint*

*bunch of fresh flat leaf parsley*

*2 spring onions*

*6 tbsp cold-pressed olive oil*

*zest and juice of 1 lemon*

*2 tbsp pomegranate molasses (honey works too)*

*½ tsp mixed spice*

*50g shelled pistachios*

*50g toasted flaked almonds (see 244)*

*seeds of 1 pomegranate*

*sea salt and black pepper*

*cont.*

If you are making the tabbouleh, prepare the buckwheat first. Place the buckwheat in a medium pan, add the mixed spice, cumin and some salt and pepper. Stir to combine before adding 450ml of water. Bring everything to the boil then reduce to a low bubble or simmer. Cook for 10–15 minutes. Keep an eye on it as you don't want it to burn – you may need to add a touch more water.

Whilst the buckwheat is cooking you can prepare the koftas. Set aside about half the coriander leaves and finely chop the remaining leaves and the stems. In a medium bowl, combine the turkey mince, onion, apricots, cumin, mixed spice, chopped coriander, lemon zest and some salt and pepper and shape into 8 koftas with your hands. Let these rest while you return to the tabbouleh.

When most of the water in the tabbouleh pan has been absorbed, turn off the heat, cover the saucepan and allow the buckwheat to sit for a further 5 minutes. It should be cooked but still have bite. Transfer it to a bowl and allow it to cool. You could also transfer it to a wide plate to allow it to cool faster.

Chop the mint, parsley, remaining coriander and spring onions. Set a small handful of herbs aside. Add the remaining chopped herbs, onion, olive oil, lemon zest and juice, pomegranate molasses, mixed spice, pistachios, flaked almonds, about half of the pomegranate seeds, and as much lemon juice as suits your taste to the cooled tabbouleh and season to taste.

cont.

***For the koftas***

*bunch of coriander, leaves roughly separated from stems*

*450g free-range turkey mince*

*½ red onion, finely chopped*

*50g organic, dried apricots, sulphur dioxide-free, finely chopped*

*½ tsp ground cumin*

*½ tsp mixed spice*

*zest and juice of 1 lemon*

*rapeseed oil or coconut oil, for greasing*

***For the tahini dressing***

*6 tbsp tahini*

*3 tbsp pomegranate molasses*

*3 tbsp cold-pressed olive oil*

*2 tbsp apple cider vinegar*

Combine all the tahini dressing ingredients together, adding as much water as necessary to achieve a thick glossy dressing. Add more molasses or vinegar as suits your taste and set aside whilst you cook your koftas.

Light the barbecue or preheat the grill and lightly oil a roasting tray. Place the koftas on the tray and grill for 10–12 minutes, turning halfway through.

Divide the tabbouleh among four plates, if using, and place the warm koftas on top. Drizzle with a little of the tahini dressing and sprinkle over the remaining herbs and pomegranate seeds.

What I love most about this dish is its colour; naturally bright and golden (hence the name), it never fails to create a few wide-eyed 'wows' at the table. The saffron adds a celebratory element to it and has a wonderfully aromatic effect as it cooks. Any leftovers are delicious cold and I often make extra for this reason.

# Celebration golden chicken *with spinach and mint*

**Serves 4**

*2 tbsp olive oil*

*800g skinless, boneless chicken thighs or mini breast fillets*

*1 leek, very finely chopped*

*1 tsp turmeric*

*good pinch of saffron*

*1 tsp ground ginger*

*250ml chicken or vegetable stock (or dissolve 2 low-sodium cubes or 2 tbsp stock powder into 250ml water)*

*250g spinach leaves, washed*

*sea salt and black pepper*

*handful of mint leaves, to serve*

*50g pistachios, roughly chopped (or toasted hazelnuts, flaked almonds), to serve*

Heat half the oil in a pan and sauté the chicken until slightly browned – you don't want to cook it through completely. Once the chicken has gained a nice colour, remove from the pan and set aside.

Add the leek, turmeric, saffron, ginger and the remaining oil to the pan and slightly soften the leek before adding the stock.

Return the chicken to the pan, cover and simmer on a low–medium temperature for 20 minutes. Keep a close eye on it as you may want to add more water if you feel it is cooking too quickly. Conversely, if you find the chicken is cooking quicker than the water is absorbing, remove the lid for the last 7–10 minutes to help the water evaporate off slightly. Once the water is absorbed and the chicken is cooked through but is still tender, add the spinach, covering the pan again immediately to let the spinach wilt.

Once the spinach has wilted, serve the chicken sprinkled with the mint and pistachios (or nut of choice).

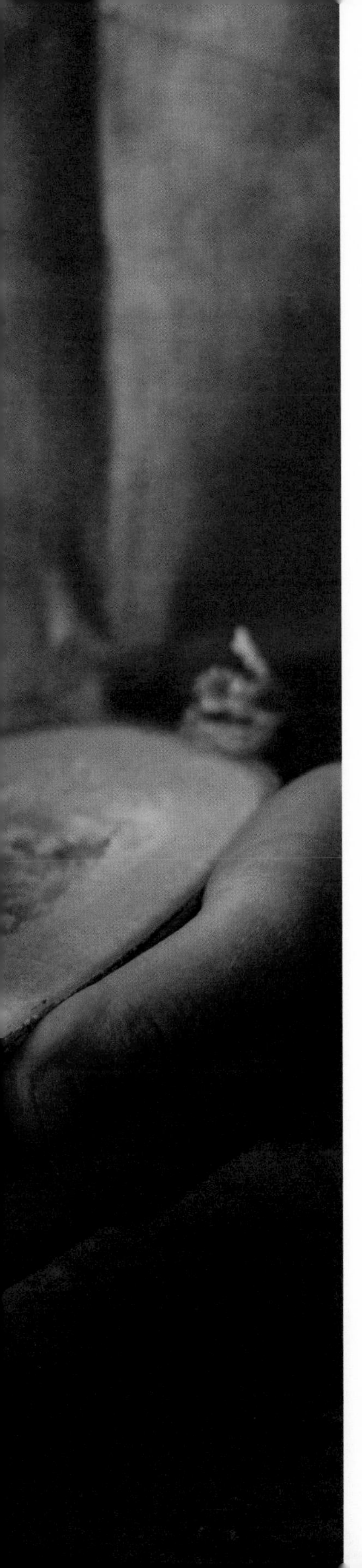

# Making vegetable king

This was one of the chapters that I most looked forward to writing. Although I am not entirely vegetarian there is nothing that excites me more than seeing so many brilliant chefs, restaurants and publications devoted to vegetable dishes, proving that vegetarian food can be just as delicious as its meaty counterpart. I tend to cook purely with vegetables at least three times a week, and when entertaining, I find it quite easy to please both veggies and meat-eaters. Very often, even if we are eating a little fish or meat with our meal the vegetable dishes will still be the centrepiece. As well as being delicious this is a far more sustainable way of eating, and whilst I don't condone dietary restrictions, I do believe that by eating a little less meat we will be doing our planet a service. In the spirit of that approach, this chapter features recipes in which the vegetables take centre stage. The dishes are so hearty and satisfying that even the most dedicated carnivore will hopefully be sated and content!

Radishes get a poor hand when it comes to their share of recipes, mainly being reserved for salads and crudités. But while I love them in both, I cannot recommend them enough enjoyed hot out of the oven. Roasting seems to balance out their pepperiness, adding a mouthwatering sweetness that produces little pink balloons full of flavour. As well as being delicious, with a pleasantly wild taste, this pesto is rather a clever way of making use of the whole radish, so there is no waste.

# Black rice risotto

*with roasted radishes and radish leaf pesto*

**Serves 2**

***For the risotto***

*1 tbsp butter or coconut oil*

*1 garlic clove, finely chopped*

*1 large shallot, finely chopped*

*200g black risotto rice*

*1 tbsp honey*

*1 litre chicken or vegetable stock*

*sea salt and black pepper*

***For the roasted radishes***

*2 bunches of radishes with leaves, washed and cut in half*

*2 tbsp olive oil*

*2 tbsp lemon juice (about ½ a lemon)*

*2 tsp honey*

***For the pesto***

*leaves of 2 bunches of radish (see above)*

*1 small garlic clove, roughly chopped*

Begin by separating your radish leaves from the bulbs. Wash the leaves and pat them dry with a clean tea towel.

Place the radish leaves, garlic, pine nuts, basil, olive oil and lemon zest in a food processor and give it a few quick pulses until you have reached the desired consistency – you may need to use a spatula to push the leaves down. I like a relatively chunky pesto. For a saucier pesto, add more olive oil and a squeeze of lemon juice. Season to taste and transfer to a bowl.

Preheat the oven to 180°C/350°F/gas mark 4. Combine the radishes in a bowl with the olive oil, lemon juice, honey and some salt and pepper before spreading in one layer in a baking tray. Roast for about 20 minutes or until sticky and slightly charred.

Meanwhile, start the risotto. Place the butter or coconut oil, garlic and shallot in a large frying pan and gently stir over a medium heat for about 5 minutes until everything has softened. If it is browning too quickly, reduce the heat and add a couple of tablespoons of water.

Pour in the rice, 1 tablespoon of water and season with a little salt and pepper. Reduce the heat to a gentle simmer and toss the rice in the pan for 5–10 minutes. Keep an eye on it as you don't want the rice to burn, but after about 7 minutes it should begin to give off a wonderfully nutty aroma. Now add the honey and 200ml of the stock. Stir and allow the rice to gently absorb the liquid before adding another 100–150ml of stock. Keep adding small amounts of stock until the rice has cooked through and begun to take on a slightly sticky texture. It is important to keep the risotto moving; I like to stir it roughly every 10 minutes.

*70g pine nuts*

*large handful of basil leaves*

*5 tbsp cold-pressed olive oil*

*zest of ½ lemon*

The risotto usually takes 40 minutes–1 hour to cook, but keep checking it. When cooked the risotto should be slightly sticky but still have some bite.

To serve, divide among serving plates and top with 2 generous tablespoons of the radish leaf pesto, followed by the roasted radishes. Serve warm.

Inspired by the classic French tarte Tatin, this dish is baked upside down before being flipped over, ready to eat. I don't think I will ever lose the pre-tart-turning nerves nor the sheer joy when I unveil the shining jewelled masterpiece! I like to serve this at big summer lunches on a bright blue serving plate to contrast with the orange of the carrots, usually with a handful of colourful salads (pages 178–180) and a Herby yoghurt sauce (page 140) or my savoury Cashew cream (page 231).

# Carrot tarte Tatin

*with olive oil pastry*

**Serves 6–8**

*4 tbsp olive oil, plus extra for greasing*

*about 7 tbsp light brown soft sugar or coconut sugar*

*500g carrots (about 9–10) peeled and chopped about ½cm thick*

*1 large banana shallot or 2 small ones, finely sliced*

*1 tsp harissa spice*

*½ tsp mixed spice*

*1 tbsp balsamic vinegar*

*sea salt and black pepper*

*savoury Cashew cream (page 231) or Herby yoghurt sauce (page 140), to serve (optional)*

*cont.*

Line the base of a 20cm round cake tin with baking parchment, allowing the paper to go just slightly up the sides, then grease with olive oil. Sprinkle 1 tablespoon of the sugar over the base of the tin and shake it to distribute it evenly – this helps add that extra caramel colour to the tart.

Blanch the carrots in a pan of boiling water for about 3 minutes, then drain.

In a large frying pan, place 2 tablespoons of the olive oil, the chopped shallots, half the harissa and 1 tablespoon of sugar over a low–medium heat. I always add a couple of tablespoons of water to prevent the shallots from burning. Once softened, remove the shallots and let them cool.

Add 2 tablespoons of olive oil to the same pan that you cooked the shallots in along with the remaining ½ teaspoon of harissa, the mixed spice, balsamic vinegar, sugar and 3 tablespoons of water. Using a wooden spatula, combine these ingredients then tip in the carrots. Coat the carrots in the caramel for about 5 minutes, stirring, keeping the temperature at a medium heat. Once all the carrots are coated, increase the heat until the carrots sing you a little sizzle from the pan. You want to give them a nice char, so give the pan a shake about every 5 minutes, and continue to cook for 15–20 minutes. Once nicely coloured and sticky, remove the carrots from the heat and allow to cool slightly while you get on with the pastry.

cont.

***For the pastry***

*150g plain, spelt or gluten-free blend flour*

*60g ground almonds*

*100ml olive oil*

*50ml cold water*

***Herby yoghurt sauce (optional)***

*2 heaped tbsp finely chopped mint leaves*

*150g organic cow, goat or sheep's yoghurt or coconut yoghurt*

*zest of 1 lemon, juice of ½ lemon*

To make the pastry, put the flour, almonds and a pinch of salt in a large bowl and using a whisk or wooden spoon, mix until combined. Make sure you remove any lumps – you may need to use the back of your spoon to crush any almond clumps. Add the olive oil followed by the cold water and using a metal spoon continue to mix until you form a slightly sticky pastry. Set aside while you return to the carrots.

Using your hands, cover the base of the tin with the carrots, charred side down. Place the smaller carrot rounds down first, using the larger ones to fill the gaps. Ideally you don't want to see any of the baking parchment below. Then spread the shallots evenly over the carrots.

Preheat the oven to 180°C/350°F/gas mark 4.

Placing the pastry ball between two pieces of baking parchment, roll it out to a circular shape no larger than your tin. This pastry has a delicate texture and is easily breakable so you don't want to roll it too thin. Remove the top layer of parchment from the pastry, then slide your hand underneath the sheet lining its bottom and, working quickly, flip it over the top of the carrot-lined tray. This is easier if you are using a shallow cake tin but even then it can a break. Don't panic, the look of this tart is rustic and no one sees the bottom anyway. Use your fingers and thumbs to gently marry any disconnected pastry together, making the tucked-down edges a little thicker to give the tart more strength.

Place the tart in the oven and bake for 35–40 minutes until the pastry has turned a nice golden colour and is hard to the touch. Remove from the oven and allow to cool slightly.

And finally, it's the pinnacle moment. Place your serving plate of choice over the top of the crust and in one swift, confident movement, flip the tart. Remove the tin and the lining paper and give yourself a pat on the back.

To make the minted yoghurt, simply combine the mint leaves with the yoghurt, lemon zest and juice and a pinch of salt. Serve with the tart. Or you could serve it with my savoury Cashew cream (see page 231).

The tart will keep well in the fridge for three days but I wouldn't keep it much longer or the bottom will lose its crispness.

A traditional Swiss dish, the rosti is similar to an oversized hash brown. I like to use a variety of root vegetables in mine – usually the odd parsnips and potatoes that didn't get cooked for Sunday lunch. You can peel the skin off your potatoes but I rather like its flavour. I tend to serve this with three or four trimmings, such as leftover chicken and a few crunchy and quick salads: my Toasted almond, rocket and parsley salad being a favourite (see page 229) and sometimes a couple of fried eggs for more of a traditional approach.

# Root vegetable sharing rosti

*with all the trimmings*

**Serves 4**

*2 medium sweet or ordinary potatoes, cut in half*

*1 shallot, finely sliced*

*1 tbsp dried thyme*

*2 carrots, peeled and grated*

*2 parsnips, peeled and grated*

*about 4 good tbsp butter or coconut oil*

*sea salt and freshly ground black pepper*

***To serve***

*200g cold, shredded chicken (leftover from Sunday lunch), drizzled with olive oil and lemon juice to taste*

*roasted vine tomatoes*

*large bunch of spinach wilted in a pan with avocado and yellow pepper smash (page 180)*

*Toasted almond, rocket and parsley salad (page 229)*

Parboil the potatoes until they are just tender but not soft. Sweet potatoes will take less time than ordinary potatoes. Drain, then plunge them into a bowl of ice-cold water and allow them to cool. If you have time, chill them in the fridge for a couple of hours, then grate them.

Stir the shallot, thyme and salt and pepper into the grated potatoes with the grated carrot and parsnips.

Melt half the butter or coconut oil in a large frying pan and add the grated vegetables in little piles, tossing them a little in the oil before patting them down lightly to form a flat cake. Try not to press down too hard. Cook over a medium heat for about 12 minutes, giving the pan a little shake every so often.

Place a large plate on top of the pan and invert the rosti onto it, then melt the remaining butter or oil in the pan and slide the rosti back in to cook the other side. Cook for 10–12 minutes then slide the rosti back onto the plate.

Place the rosti in the centre of the table alongside your favourite sides, leaving everyone to serve themselves.

The poor marrow is too often labelled as the failure of the vegetable patch. True, when left too long it can have a bitter and watery taste, but if picked when medium-sized it can be scrumptious. Sweet peppers and nutty lentils play nicely with the sharpness of the cheese here, all topped off with the perkiness of basil. I like to use both the stem and leaf of the basil here, so that none of the herb is wasted. For a vegan version, you can omit the feta cheese.

# Fiery lentil-stuffed marrow boats

**Serves 4**

*1 medium marrow*

*4 tbsp olive oil, plus extra for coating*

*3 red peppers, halved, deseeded and finely sliced*

*2 shallots, finely sliced*

*2 garlic cloves, crushed*

*250g cherry tomatoes, halved*

*150g Puy lentils (uncooked weight), cooked according to packet instructions*

*2 tbsp tomato purée mixed with 2 tbsp harissa paste*

*1 tsp cayenne pepper*

*½ tsp paprika*

*1 red chilli, deseeded and finely chopped*

*bunch of basil, leaves separated from stems*

*70g feta cheese*

*handful of toasted almonds, chopped (see page 244)*

*sea salt and black pepper*

Preheat the oven to 180°C/350°F/gas mark 4.

Slice the marrow in half lengthways and scoop out the very watery seedy part. Rub the marrow with olive oil and a little salt, place on a roasting tray and bake for about 20 minutes or until it has started to brown and is cooked through.

Meanwhile, place about 2 tablespoons of olive oil in a frying pan and cook the peppers and shallot on a medium heat until the shallots are soft and the peppers have started to char. Add the garlic and halved cherry tomatoes. Cook until your tomatoes have softened (about 10–12 minutes). If the garlic is browning too quickly, add a tablespoon or so of water.

Lower the heat and add the cooked lentils, a further 2 tablespoons of olive oil, the combined tomato purée-harissa paste, cayenne pepper, paprika and chilli, then continue to cook and let the flavours infuse for 3–5 minutes. Remove from the heat. Chop the basil stems to roughly ½ cm pieces and add these to the pan. Crumble in about half of your feta, if using, then stir to combine and season to taste.

Once the marrow is cooked, remove from the oven and fill the centres with the lentil mix. Drizzle with a little more olive oil and if you are using the feta, sprinkle the remainder over the top. Return to the oven for a further 20 minutes or until the lentils or feta have crisped up slightly and the marrow has gone golden brown.

Transfer to a serving plate and give the marrow a good drizzle of olive oil, scatter with the toasted almonds and tear over the basil leaves before serving.

I love the aromatic flavour of thyme and it works perfectly in this quiche. Ricotta has a delicate taste which I adore but you could add a little grated Parmesan if you are looking for that tang. The pastry has a good nuttiness to it and uses oats and toasted seeds in the place of flour, making it a little less elastic than conventional pastry. I've found pushing it into the tin by hand works better than using a rolling pin and it also leaves you one less utensil to wash up, which is never a bad thing.

# Leek, thyme and ricotta quiche

*with toasted seed and oat crust*

**Serves 8–10**

***For the crust***

*200g jumbo oats*

*good pinch of salt*

*60g sunflower seeds, toasted (see page 244)*

*80g chilled butter, cubed (or coconut oil – chilled in the fridge until very cold), plus 1 tbsp for frying*

*4–5 tbsp ice-cold water*

*250g leeks (roughly 2 large leeks), sliced on a diagonal into roughly 1cm slices*

*2 garlic cloves, crushed or finely chopped*

*handful of spinach leaves*

*4 large eggs (5 if using medium)*

*100ml organic milk or unsweetened non-dairy milk (such as almond or oat)*

*pinch of turmeric*

Place the oats and a good pinch of salt in a food processor and pulse until you have a flour. Add the toasted sunflower seeds and pulse a few times until the seeds resemble a crumb-like coarse flour. Don't over-blend as you want to keep a little texture.

Add the chilled butter or oil and pulse until the mixture resembles coarse breadcrumbs. Slowly add the water until the mixture begins to form a rough dough. You may want to transfer it to a bowl and finish using your hands. Shape the dough into a disc and wrap it in cling film, then transfer to the fridge for about an hour, or you could place it in the freezer for 15 minutes.

While the dough is chilling, preheat the oven to 190°C/375°F/gas mark 5. Transfer the leeks and 1 tablespoon of butter or coconut oil to the frying pan and cook on a low–medium heat until soft. Add the garlic and continue to stir everything for a minute or so. Add the spinach and cook for a further minute or until it has wilted. Remove the pan from the heat.

Take the dough from the fridge or freezer and press it down into the tart tin to an even thickness. Persevere with this – if your tart shell is the correct size there will be enough pastry. Make sure you give your sides strength rather than focusing on a heavy base. Prick the base of the pastry shell and bake in the oven for about 10 minutes or until the pastry has dried out a little. Remove and set aside. Reduce the oven temperature to about 170°C/325°F/gas mark 3.

*1–2 tbsp freshly picked thyme leaves*

*100g fresh ricotta cheese*

*3–4 tbsp grated Parmesan cheese (optional)*

*sea salt and black pepper*

***You will need a 25cm non-stick, loose-bottomed tart tin***

In a medium bowl, whisk together the eggs, milk, turmeric, thyme and a pinch of salt and pepper using a fork. Add the leeks and spinach and combine. Add about half the ricotta, breaking it up where you can and loosely stirring it in. If you are using Parmesan, stir it in at this point, too.

Pour the mixture into the pastry shell and crumble or spoon over the remaining ricotta and another pinch of salt. Bake for 30–45 minutes or until the middle of the quiche has set but has a slight wobble. Remove and leave the quiche to cool completely before serving.

The filling of this delicious tart is rich and flavoursome, and the turmeric adds a glorious golden effect to the crumbly pastry. To make it wholly vegetarian, the anchovies can happily be excluded. Ideally this should be served cold so that once it has had time to firm up a little. It goes down very well at any summer picnic or dinner party and keeps for up to five days, making it a packed lunch contender, too. I like to serve mine with some abundant colourful salads (pages 178–180) or dips such as my Black olive tapenade (page 238) and some toasted bread.

# Roasted red pepper tart

*with turmeric almond crust*

**Serves 8–10**

***For the pastry***

*250g ground almonds*

*1 tbsp flour of choice (gluten-free blend, or rice, oat, quinoa or spelt flour)*

*½ tsp turmeric*

*½ tsp cayenne pepper*

*2 eggs, lightly beaten*

*2 tbsp melted coconut oil*

***For the filling***

*5 red peppers, deseeded and roughly chopped*

*1 unpeeled garlic clove, base chopped off*

*coconut or rapeseed oil, for roasting*

*550g large tomatoes*

*1 tbsp tomato purée*

*1 tsp cayenne pepper*

*2 anchovy fillets, rinsed (optional)*

*3 eggs, whisked well*

*sea salt and black pepper*

Preheat the oven to 200°C/400°F/gas mark 6 and lightly grease the sides of the tart tin, then line the base with baking parchment.

Place the peppers and garlic on a large baking tray and rub them in a little oil, then season with salt and pepper. Roast for 20–25 minutes until softened and charred. Set aside and lower the oven temperature to 180°C/350°F/gas mark 4.

Prepare the tomatoes by removing any stems and slice an X in the bottom of each. Place them in a saucepan, cover them in just boiled water and leave for about 5 minutes. Prepare a bowl of ice-cold water, then transfer the tomatoes using a slotted spoon into the ice-cold water. Once they are cool, peel away the skin, starting at the X. Chop the tomatoes in half or quarters and remove their watery seedy centres – I usually throw these into a stock.

To make the pastry, combine the ground almonds, flour, turmeric, cayenne and a pinch of salt in a large bowl. Stir in the eggs and melted coconut oil. You could use a food processor for this, but I prefer the hands-on approach.

Using your fingers, press the pastry into the tin, going right to the edges and leaving absolutely no holes. Prick the base of the pastry all over using a fork and bake for about 12 minutes, until slightly dried out. Remove from the oven and raise the oven temperature to 190°C/375°F/gas mark 5.

Squeeze the roasted garlic from the skin. It should come out a little like toothpaste. If it is still slightly raw, do not worry as it is all going to be mixed up anyway. Transfer

*1 tbsp chopped basil, to serve*

*drizzle of cold-pressed olive oil, to serve*

***You will need a 24cm non-stick, loose-bottomed, tart tin***

the garlic, roasted peppers, peeled tomatoes, tomato purée, cayenne, anchovies, if using, and a good grind of salt and pepper to a food processor. Blitz until there are no lumps remaining. Add the eggs and pulse again until well combined.

Place the tart shell on the middle rack in the oven and pull it out as far as you comfortably can. Slowly pour the filling into the shell then slide back into the oven and bake for 35–40 minutes. The filling should be set but with a slight wobble. It's best to let the tart cool completely before serving but an hour or so will do. Serve with a sprinkle of torn basil, freshly ground black pepper and drizzle with a little olive oil.

Of all the places in the world that I've visited, the Greek islands are probably my favourite. I love the people, the sea, the way the villages and towns stay alive with children playing in the streets until the very early hours. Most of all, however, I love the food. Something I always look forward to whenever I find the time to travel to these beautiful islands is aubergine Imam. Rich and meaty, the aubergine is cooked slowly in a thick tomatoey sauce. This recipe is fantastic as both a summer or winter dish and works both as a side and a vegetarian main.

## Baked aubergine Imam

**Serves 4 as a main, 6–8 as a side**

*rapeseed or coconut oil, for frying*

*2 medium onions, finely sliced*

*3 garlic cloves, crushed*

*400g tin of chopped tomatoes*

*1 box/bunch of cherry tomatoes (about 250g), cut in half*

*1 tbsp dried thyme*

*2 tbsp chopped parsley, plus extra to serve*

*3 tbsp olive oil*

*3 large aubergines or 4 smaller ones, cut lengthways into 1cm slices*

*sea salt and black pepper*

*sourdough loaf, to serve*

Preheat the oven to 180°C/350°F/gas mark 4.

Heat about 1 tablespoon of oil in a large frying pan and cook the onions until softened. You may want to add a little water to prevent the onions burning. Add the garlic, tinned tomatoes, cherry tomatoes, thyme, parsley and salt and pepper and simmer for about 10 minutes.

In a separate pan, brush the aubergine slices with a little olive oil and lightly fry them on both sides to give them some colour. You do not need to cook them through completely.

Once evenly browned, remove the aubergine slices and arrange them to cover the bottom of a deep, rectangular ovenproof dish (measuring about 20 x 20cm, 4cm deep). Cover this with a layer of the tomato sauce, then repeat this layering with more aubergine and tomato sauce. You may find you have two layers or three depending on the dimensions of your pan, but finish with a layer of tomato sauce. Put in the oven and bake for 40–45 minutes.

This dish is delicious served hot or cold and goes wonderfully well with the sourdough to mop up the sauce.

Soba noodles are one of my saviour ingredients, and something I always make sure I have in my cupboard. This recipe is perfect for when you need a good wholesome meal and you need it fast. The simple chestnut mushroom works wonderfully in this dish and adds a rich meatiness to it. You can be quite free with your choice of greenery; Tenderstem broccoli, mangetout and green beans all work well. I like to scatter my noodles with lots of chilli, fresh herbs and a generous sprinkle of sesame seeds.

# Sesame soba noodles

*with sticky miso mushrooms*

**Serves 4**

*250g brown rice soba noodles*

*knob of coconut oil*

*1 garlic clove, crushed or finely chopped*

*thumb-sized piece of ginger, peeled and grated or finely chopped*

*300g Tenderstem broccoli, roughly cut on a diagonal (or mangetout, green beans)*

*1–2 handfuls of spinach leaves*

*3 tbsp sesame seeds (toasted or untoasted)*

***For the mushrooms***

*1 heaped tbsp melted coconut oil or rapeseed oil*

*2 tbsp brown rice miso paste*

*1 tsp apple cider vinegar*

*1 tsp toasted sesame oil*

Preheat the oven to 200°C/400°F/gas mark 6 and line a small baking dish with baking parchment.

First prepare the mushrooms. Combine the melted coconut oil, miso paste, vinegar, sesame oil and honey in a medium bowl, then add the mushrooms and coat them in the miso mix using your hands. Tip into the baking dish and roast for about 25 minutes, tossing halfway through.

While the mushrooms are in the oven, quickly cook the soba noodles following the packet instructions – usually 5–6 minutes. Drain and rinse in cold water.

In a large frying pan, melt a knob of coconut oil and cook the garlic and ginger for about 1 minute. Add the broccoli and cook for about 3 minutes, tossing it in the ginger and garlic. Add the spinach, allowing it to wilt slightly before stirring in the soba noodles.

Combine the dressing ingredients in a small bowl, then pour into the pan along with the sesame seeds and stir through.

Divide the noodles evenly among individual plates and top with the sticky miso mushrooms and whatever garnish you are using; coriander, freshly chopped chilli and toasted sesame seeds is always a delicious combination.

*1 tbsp honey*

*500g chestnut mushrooms, cut in half, or quarters if large*

***For the dressing***

*2 tbsp cold-pressed olive oil*

*1 tsp toasted sesame oil*

*juice of 1 lemon*

*4 tbsp tamari*

*4 tbsp almond or peanut butter (smooth if possible)*

*1 tbsp honey or maple syrup (optional)*

***To garnish***

*Toasted sesame seeds (page 245)*

*Toasted cashews (page 244)*

*Chopped coriander*

*Diced red chillies*

A firm British favourite, shepherd's pie is comfort food at its best and this meat-free version is just as satisfying and full of flavour as the classic. Feel free to use whatever vegetables are in season and to swap in other herbs. This recipe uses classic Mediterranean flavours celebrating basil and thyme, but for a more spice-rich one, try my Moroccan pie over the page. I use a creamy cauliflower topping for my pies as I prefer the lighter taste but you can use good old-fashioned mashed potato if you prefer.

# Shepherdless pie

**Serves 4–6**

*3 leeks, chopped on the diagonal roughly 1cm in width*

*olive oil, butter or coconut oil*

*2 garlic cloves, crushed or finely chopped*

*2 courgettes, thinly sliced*

*400g tin organic chopped tomatoes*

*1 tbsp fresh thyme leaves*

*handful of cavalo nero, chopped into 1cm ribbons, or 2 handfuls spinach or kale*

*4 large plum vine tomatoes, quartered*

*large bunch of basil*

***For the topping***

*2 cauliflower heads, chopped*

*2 tbsp tahini*

*2 tsp Dijon mustard*

Preheat the oven to 200°C/400°F/gas mark 6.

First, make the topping. Bring a large pan of water to the boil and cook the cauliflower until soft, 5–8 minutes. Drain and return to the pan before mashing the cauliflower until it is as smooth as you can get it. I use a stick blender for this but a simple potato masher is fine. Add the tahini, Dijon mustard, salt and pepper. Stir everything together and check the seasoning, adjusting if necessary.

Place the leeks and one knob of butter or oil in a large, deep frying pan over a medium heat and toss, allowing them to brown a little. Add a few tablespoons of water to help them soften and cook until soft, about 5 minutes. Add the garlic and cook for another minute.

Add the courgettes and a little more oil or butter, tossing everything to make sure the courgettes are coated. Cook for about 5 minutes or until the courgettes are just beginning to soften. Next, add the tomatoes and thyme leaves. Stir everything together and allow it to bubble away for about 8 minutes and thicken slightly.

When the vegetables are bubbling nicely, add the cavalo nero or spinach or kale, plus the tomato quarters and cook for another 2 minutes or so to wilt the cavalo nero slightly. Taste and season to your liking before stirring through the basil leaves.

*sea salt and black pepper*

*handful of thyme, leaves picked*

*3 tbsp finely grated Parmesan (optional)*

***You will need an ovenproof dish roughly 20 x 30cm, or 24cm diameter if using a round dish.***

Transfer the vegetables to the ovenproof dish. Roughly flatten the surface before spreading over the cauliflower mash. Sprinkle over a few more thyme leaves and/ or Parmesan, if you wish.

Bake in the oven for 20–25 minutes or until the tomato has slightly started to bubble up the sides and the whole thing is warm right through. Serve warm.

Although this recipe uses quite a few spices, it isn't hot. What I love most about Moroccan flavours is the fusion of spices; delicately balanced between sweet and bold. This dish is perfect for cold winter nights and creates a wonderfully fragrant smell as it cooks. I like to use a mix of various root vegetables here as it makes for a lovely texture and colour.

# Moroccan root veg pie

**Serves 4–6**

*1 tsp mixed spice*

*1 tsp ground cinnamon*

*1 tsp ground cumin*

*½ tsp ground coriander*

*½ tsp smoked paprika*

*½ tsp turmeric*

*seeds from 4 cardamom pods*

*1 aubergine, cut into roughly 1cm cubes*

*olive oil, butter or coconut oil, for frying*

*1 large sweet potato, peeled and cut into roughly 1cm cubes*

*2 garlic cloves, crushed or finely chopped*

*1 carrot, grated, 2 thinly sliced*

*2 parsnips, thinly sliced*

*400g tin organic chopped tomatoes*

*4 large plum vine tomatoes, quartered*

*handful of fresh spinach leaves*

Preheat the oven to 200°C/400°F/gas mark 6.

First, make the topping. Bring a large pan of water to the boil and cook the cauliflower until soft, 5–8 minutes. Drain and return to the pan. Either with a stick blender or simple potato masher, mash the cauliflower until it is as smooth as you can get it. Add the tahini, Dijon mustard, salt and pepper. Stir everything together and check the seasoning, adjusting if necessary. Place a lid over the cauliflower to keep it warm while you prepare the rest of the vegetables.

Combine all the spices with the cardamom seeds in a small bowl to create a blend.

Place the aubergine with a knob of butter or oil into a large pan and add about a one-third of the spice mix. Toss to coat and cook for 5–8 minutes, allowing the aubergine to brown slightly – it does not need to be cooked through. Transfer to a plate.

Into the same pan, place the chopped sweet potato, remaining spice mix and another good knob of butter or oil, tossing everything well. Add about 200ml of water and allow it to part fry, part steam for about 10 minutes or until most of the water has been absorbed.

Then add the garlic, carrot and parsnip and cook for another 10 minutes until everything has slightly softened.

*For the topping*

*2 cauliflower heads, chopped*

*2 tbsp tahini*

*2 tsp Dijon mustard*

*½ tsp ground nutmeg*

*sea salt and black pepper*

*½ tsp crushed coriander seeds*

*3 tbsp finely grated Parmesan (optional)*

Pour in the tin of tomatoes, stir and allow everything to bubble away for about 8 minutes. Stir in the tomato quarters and spinach and cook for another minute or so, allowing the spinach to wilt, then taste before seasoning to your liking.

Pour the vegetables into your dish, roughly flattening the surface before spreading over the cauliflower mash. Sprinkle over the crushed coriander seeds, a few grinds of black pepper and/or Parmesan, if you wish. Bake in the oven for about 40 minutes and serve warm.

Any leftovers can be reheated slowly in an oven heated to 160°C/325°F/gas mark 3 until piping hot or even enjoyed cold.

I love the colour of this tart and it looks fabulous on the table. Both roasted and raw asparagus work well here, – roasted gives it a bit of a nuttier, richer taste. There are two ways to go with the pastry; my spelt pastry offers more of a classic base but you could also use my almond crust if you want to make this entirely gluten-free (page 146). When asparagus is not in season, wilted kale or spinach work well – just make sure you have squeezed out all of the excess liquid to avoid a watery tart.

# Asparagus and pea tart

**Serves 8–10**

***For the pastry***

*230g plain white spelt flour, plus extra for dusting*

*½ tsp sea salt*

*150g butter, chilled and cut into cubes*

*1 large egg, lightly beaten*

*2 tbsp ice-cold water*

***For the filling***

*bunch of asparagus*

*rapeseed oil or coconut oil, for roasting*

*450g peas, blanched and cooled*

*4 eggs, whisked well*

*1 garlic clove, crushed or finely chopped*

*2 tbsp olive oil*

*sea salt and black pepper*

For the pastry, whisk together the flour and salt in a large bowl. Add the cubed butter and rub it in with your hands until you have a coarse breadcrumb-like texture. Add the egg and water and bring everything together with a wooden spoon. You could also use a food processor for this, whizzing the flour, salt and butter until breadcrumb-like, then adding the egg and water and whizzing again until it forms a ball.

Roll out the pastry on a lightly floured surface, making sure it is larger than the tart tray. Line the tray, allowing any excess pastry to simply hang over the sides ,and prick the base using a fork. Place in the fridge to chill for 30 minutes.

I like to use this time to prepare the asparagus. Snap or chop off their woody ends before chopping into roughly 4cm pieces. If you are roasting the asparagus, preheat the oven to 200°C/400°F/gas mark 6. Place the asparagus on a baking tray, drizzle with oil and season with salt before roasting them for about 15 minutes or until they are slightly browned. Alternatively, blanch them in boiling hot water for 2 minutes before running them under cold water and setting them aside.

Reduce the oven temperature to 180°C/350°F/gas mark 4 or preheat it. Line the chilled pastry shell with baking parchment and fill it with either baking beans or dry rice. Bake in the oven for 15 minutes until it has dried out and is a pale golden brown. Remove the baking beans/rice and paper and carefully trim any excess pastry using a sharp knife. Return to the oven for another 10 minutes or until the pastry has completely dried out. Remove and allow it to cool slightly.

*You will need a deep 28cm loose-bottomed, non-stick tart tray. If your tart tray is not non-stick, lightly grease it before dusting it with flour.*

Reduce the oven temperature again to 150°C/300°F/gas mark 2. In a food processor, blend the peas, eggs, garlic, olive oil and salt and pepper until smooth. Pour into the tart shell and arrange the asparagus. Bake the tart for 20–25 minutes or until it has set but has a slight wobble in the middle. Allow the tart to cool completely before serving.

This tart will keep for up to 4 days if kept in the fridge.

# Sides

My mother grew up in Africa but summered in Holland – where she was born and where much of our family still lives – so our upbringing always had a European influence to it. The way we ate also reflected her roots, and when growing up our meals were made up of an array of dishes that would be set upon the table. Meal times were about sharing news and conversation as much as food, and everyone would help themselves and pass bowls and dishes around. The tradition has been echoed in my own cooking style and my table is often dotted with various vegetable accompaniments, to add a little more texture or colour to the meal.

The dishes in this chapter are designed to be shared and eaten with others, but you can easily make them the heart of the meal by increasing the quantities of ingredients. I am a big fan of cooking once and eating twice. Most leftovers will taste equally as delicious, if not more so, the next day. You can pair these with any of the main vegetable, meat and fish dishes in this book.

There was a restaurant that we used to go to as children where one of the signature dishes was a vodka and fennel risotto. The risotto was truly delicious, but because it was so boozy my parents would only let us share a portion. Even now when I pull the clear bottle off the top shelf to make this there is still that electric bolt of naughty excitement. I use rapeseed or olive oil for this as the flavour is more subtle than coconut oil, but use whatever you prefer.

# Boozy fennel with almonds

**Serves 4**

*2 medium fennel bulbs*

*2–3 tbsp rapeseed or olive oil*

*3 or more tbsp vodka*

*sea salt*

*handful of almonds, toasted (see page 244) and chopped, to serve*

Preheat the oven to 200°C/400°F/gas mark 6.

Slice the very bottom of the fennel bulbs to remove the woody stalk, then slice into roughly even slices. Transfer to a roasting pan and toss with the oil and a little salt.

Roast for 35–40 minutes or until the fennel is nicely charred. Transfer to a serving dish and while it is still warm, drizzle over the vodka and give it all a toss to coat.

Sprinkle over the toasted almonds and serve.

A wonderfully fragrant and colourful dish with Thai-inspired flavours, I love this served with some simply cooked fish or meat, either roasted or pan-fried. It keeps very well, too, so it is often enjoyed as a weekday dinner with two poached eggs on top, a few extra herbs and some chopped fresh chilli.

# Aromatic, shredded broccoli salad

**Serves 4–6**

*2 broccoli heads*

*1 garlic clove, crushed*

*1 lemongrass stalk*

*thumb-sized piece of ginger, peeled and grated*

*handful of coriander, stems roughly chopped, leaves roughly torn*

*½ green chilli, deseeded and finely chopped*

*juice of ½ lemon*

*3 tbsp cold-pressed olive oil*

*1 tbsp apple cider vinegar*

*1 tsp sesame oil*

*sea salt and black pepper*

Steam or boil the broccoli until it is 'al dente' – it should be just cooked; you should be able to pierce it only with a sharp knife. Drain and allow it to cool slightly.

In a food processor, combine the garlic, lemongrass, ginger, coriander stems, chilli and lemon juice. Pulse until combined and the stems have broken down. Add the coriander leaves, oil, vinegar, sesame oil and salt and pepper and pulse again until everything is well broken down and combined. Transfer to a large bowl.

Clean out the food processor bowl, add the broccoli and pulse until it has broken down to a 'rice'-like consistency. You may need to do this in batches. Transfer to the bowl with the spice blend, mix everything together and season to taste.

Serve immediately, or this will keep stored in the fridge in an airtight container for up to 4 days.

A brilliant way to use up any sad-looking romaine lettuce, this recipe is probably my favourite of the book. I serve this both hot and cold with this simple but effective dressing. Feel free to add a pinch of dried herbs, too, for a deeper herby taste. This is delicious with some fresh fish. I love it with my Spicy grilled squid (page 112).

# Chargrilled herby romaine hearts

**Serves 4**

*3–4 heads of romaine lettuce*

*4 tbsp olive oil*

*1 tbsp apple cider vinegar*

*zest and juice of 1 lemon*

*1 tbsp very finely chopped herbs (basil, mint, coriander and parsley will all do)*

*1 level tbsp dried mixed herbs – rosemary, oregano (optional)*

*1 tsp honey*

*1 tsp grainy mustard*

*sea salt black pepper*

Begin by pulling off any very, very sad leaves from the lettuce – a little floppy is fine but anything that has started to disintegrate should go (although you can add these to stock). Carefully remove the brown part of the root end – you want to keep the lettuce intact, so take care not to cut too far. Chop about 5cm off the top of the lettuce head, keeping these leaves for a salad or stock, then slice the romaines in half lengthways and set them on a serving platter, chopped edge down.

Mix the oil, vinegar, lemon zest, herbs (both fresh and dried), honey, mustard and a small amount of seasoning in a bowl, then, using a pastry brush, paint about one-third of the dressing over the outer leaves of the lettuce before turning them upwards and painting the remaining mix over the open halves.

Heat a grill or griddle pan to high and grill the lettuce halves for about 10 minutes or until well charred, turning halfway through.

Squeeze over a little lemon juice and serve.

This is one of my favourite ways to use up any sad-looking vegetables, such as floppy carrots or leftover peas, although I often make these recipes from young and lively vegetables, too. You can pair them with some fish or meat as an exciting and lighter alternative to mashed potato or as a replacement for a sauce. I use my trusty stick blender for this as it creates less washing up, but if you don't have one, a food processor or masher will work too.

# Four vegetable mash recipes

**Each recipe roughly serves 4**

## Basil broccoli stalk mash

*stalks of 4 broccoli, roughly chopped (or 2 whole broccoli)*

*6–8 tbsp cold-pressed olive oil*

*generous handful of basil, stems finely chopped, leaves roughly torn*

*sea salt and black pepper*

Place the broccoli stalk in a large pan and half-cover it with boiling water. Put a lid on the pan and part boil, part steam until it is soft enough that you can pierce it with a table knife.

Drain into a colander and return the broccoli stalk to the pan along with the olive oil, basil and seasoning. Blitz to a mash using your stick blender and serve either hot or cold.

This will keep in an airtight container in the fridge for up to 4 days.

# White miso cauliflower mash

*1 large or 2 medium cauliflower heads, broken into florets*

*4 tbsp white miso paste*

*2 tbsp cold-pressed olive oil or butter*

*sea salt and black pepper*

Boil or steam the cauliflower in a large pan until soft, then drain.

Either in your cooking pan or a small bowl, combine the miso, oil or butter and some seasoning with the drained cauliflower. Blitz until smooth using a stick blender and serve warm with a good grind of black pepper. Serve at once, or transfer to an airtight container once cooled and keep in the fridge for up to 4 days.

I find this is best served warm. To heat it, tip the mash into a saucepan and bring it to piping hot slowly, starting on a low heat and increasing it, stirring all the time.

# Wasabi pea mash

*900g peas (frozen is fine)*

*4 tbsp cold-pressed olive oil*

*1–2 tsp wasabi paste (or use powder mixed with water)*

*pinch of salt*

Boil the peas until cooked through, then drain.

Tip the peas into a large bowl and add the olive oil, a little wasabi and a pinch of salt, then blitz using your stick blender until smooth, adding more olive oil if needed, or if you prefer you can leave a few broken peas for more of a rough texture. Serve hot or cold. This will keep in an airtight container in the fridge for up to 4 days.

# Moroccan carrot mash

*900g–1kg carrots, peeled and roughly chopped*

*4 tbsp cold-pressed, extra-virgin olive oil*

*3 tbsp tahini*

*1 tsp mixed spice*

*1 tsp harissa spice or cayenne or chilli pepper or paprika*

*sea salt and black pepper*

Steam or boil the carrots until soft enough that they can be pierced with a table knife.

Transfer the cooked carrots to a large bowl, add the olive oil, tahini, mixed spice and harissa or alternative and blitz until smooth using a stick blender. Season to taste and blitz again or stir.

Serve the mash hot or cold. This will keep in an airtight container in the fridge for up to 4 days.

Corn on the cob is one of my favourite comfort foods. There is something about the act of eating with my hands that brings me right back to six o'clock teatime, bath and bed. Although a recognised childhood favourite, this recipe is full of complex and mature flavours that give it that little bit extra. You can, of course, take a more dainty approach and slice the kernels off with a knife, but for me the best and only way is the messy way. You can use either a griddle pan or barbecue for this.

# Miso-butter corn

**Serves 4**

*3 tbsp white or brown miso paste*

*4 tbsp butter (or coconut oil), melted, plus extra for grilling*

*a good squeeze of fresh lime or lemon juice*

*a few good grinds of freshly ground black pepper*

*a pinch of cayenne pepper*

*4 ears of corn, husks on*

*2 spring onions, roughly chopped, to serve*

*2 tbsp toasted sesame seeds (see page 245), to serve*

To make the miso-butter, place the miso paste and butter in a bowl with the lime or lemon juice, pepper and cayenne pepper and mix until you have a paste. If you are using coconut oil and it is solid, you can melt it before adding it to the miso, but you may want to place it back in the fridge for 20 minutes or so once you have made up the paste, just so that you have more of a paste than a dressing.

Now prepare the corn. I like to just pull back the husks of the corn and use them to turn the corn on the grill. Rub the corn with a little more butter and season with just a pinch of salt. Grill over a medium–high heat for about 5 minutes, turning as necessary.

Once cooked, spread the corn with a generous amount of the miso-butter paste and serve warm, sprinkled with spring onions and sesame seeds.

Potato gratin is one of the ultimate comfort foods. I first tried it one very special holiday in the Swiss Alps and thought it was just genius! I make mine with sweet potato and lots of fresh rosemary or thyme for a herby flavour. Ricotta gives it a lighter twist than the traditional Gruyère, but this dish is still wonderfully rich and indulgent – perfect for a rainy Sunday or a wintery evening. Serve it alongside some roasted fish or chicken, or enjoy it simply as it is with a little side salad.

# Ricotta and sweet potato gratin

**Serves 4–6**

*about 100g butter or coconut oil, plus extra for greasing*

*2 shallots, finely chopped*

*bunch or bag of spinach leaves (approx. 300g)*

*500g fresh ricotta*

*zest and juice of 1 lemon*

*4 tbsp fresh thyme or rosemary, chopped*

*4 sweet potatoes, peeled and cut into thin rounds*

*knob of Parmesan, grated (optional)*

*sea salt and black pepper*

Preheat the oven to 200°C/400°F/gas mark 6.

Melt the butter or coconut oil in a large pan, then add the shallots and allow them to soften. Once soft, add the spinach along with 1 tablespoon of water and a good pinch of salt. Place the lid on and turn the heat off, leaving the spinach to wilt.

After 5 minutes, lift the lid and give the spinach a stir to help it break down and combine with the shallots. If some of the leaves are still quite raw, gently turn on the heat and stir a little until fully wilted. Allow this to sit for a few minutes, then drain through a sieve. Use a spoon to press down on the leaves and push through all excess water.

In a small bowl, whisk together the ricotta, lemon zest and juice along with 3 tablespoons of your chopped herbs until the cheese has thinned a little and is as smooth as you can get it.

Lightly grease a deep 20cm square or round ovenproof dish and arrange a layer of potato rounds on the bottom. Spread over one-third of the spinach-shallot mix as evenly as you can and spoon over about one-third of the ricotta mix. Repeat this twice, finishing with a final layer of potato. Divide the butter or coconut oil evenly around the dish and sprinkle over a generous amount of salt and pepper, the rest of the thyme or rosemary, and Parmesan, if using.

Bake for about an hour or until the sides of the bake begin to bubble and the top has browned slightly. You should be able to pierce the potatoes easily with a knife. Serve warm.

Although really no more difficult than making very simple roasted potatoes, the hasselback method does create a lovely visual effect. The best thing about these is that there are no fights over who gets the crispy potatoes, for each one should be as crispy as the next. I've given the option of butter or rapeseed oil here as I find the subtler flavour lends itself best to this recipe, but you can use coconut oil if you wish.

## Hasselback baby potatoes with herby oil

**Serves 6**

*about 1kg baby new or Charlotte potatoes*

*rapeseed oil or butter, for roasting*

*good-quality flaky sea salt*

***For the herby oil***

*bunch of basil stems and leaves, finely chopped*

*bunch of coriander or parsley, leaves finely chopped*

*6–8 tbsp olive oil*

*1 tbsp cider vinegar*

*sea salt and black pepper*

Preheat the oven to 200°C/400°F/gas mark 6.

Wash and pat dry the potatoes with kitchen paper, then cut thin incisions along the length of the potato, cutting about two-thirds of the way through. Take care not to cut right through, but don't panic if you lose a few ends.

Place the hasselbacked potatoes in a large roasting pan and rub them with oil or butter. If the butter is cold, place the tray over the hob to allow it to melt first, then turn the potatoes over in the fat to coat.

Sprinkle with a generous amount of flaky sea salt and roast in the oven for about 50 minutes–1 hour, giving the tray a shake every now and then. The potatoes are cooked when the flesh is soft and the outside has crisped up nicely.

To make the herby oil, simply mix all the ingredients in a small bowl, season to taste and serve alongside or spooned over the potatoes.

This dish steals its flavour from my favourite trip to Rome. I fell in love with a caponata dish at one of the little restaurants and we must have visited it at least three times in the few days that we were there. The plump, juicy sultanas paired with the aubergine and pine nuts made me truly jealous of the local Italians, who could eat this to their hearts content. Naturally, I wanted to bring the flavours back home to my own kitchen, where I turned it into a quick jam. I love roasting cauliflower and am of the opinion that it is by far the best way to enjoy it. This dish is delicious both hot or cold and keeps very well too.

# Roasted lemon cauliflower

*with sesame seeds and quick aubergine jam*

**Serves 4–6**

*handful of sultanas, soaked overnight and drained*

*2 cauliflower heads, chopped into even-sized pieces (use the stalk too)*

*3 lemons*

*3 tbsp coconut oil, olive or rapeseed oil, plus extra for the jam*

*1 aubergine, chopped into 1cm cubes*

*8 soft, pitted dates*

*½ tsp mixed spice*

*½ tsp ground cinnamon*

*sea salt and freshly ground black pepper*

*2–3 tbsp sesame seeds, I like a mix of black and white, toasted (see page 245), to serve*

If you haven't had time to soak your sultanas, begin by softening them in a saucepan with a couple of tablespoons of water, and then warm them over a low heat until they have plumped up and absorbed the water.

Preheat the oven to 180°C/350°F/gas mark 4.

Place the cauliflower on a large roasting tray. Zest just one of your lemons over the cauliflower and sprinkle over half of its juice. Add 2 tablespoons of the oil and massage it all together using your hands. Finely slice the remaining 2 lemons and arrange them on top of the cauliflower. Season with salt and pepper and roast for about 35 minutes or until the cauliflower is cooked and has started to char.

While the cauliflower is cooking, add the remaining oil to a large frying pan and add the aubergine chunks. Stir them to toss them in the oil, as they will suck up the moisture quickly. Cook over a medium heat until they are beginning to soften. If you feel they are beginning to burn, add a little water to help them steam.

Meanwhile, break up the dates into a small saucepan and add about 100ml water as well as the spices and a pinch of salt. Allow the dates to break down, stirring and pushing them down with a wooden spoon – you should end up with a textured loose paste. You may want to add a little more water. When the aubergine is cooked, transfer it to the dates saucepan along with the juicy sultanas and cook for a further 3 minutes, stirring until well combined. I like to use the back of my spoon to break down some of the aubergine to achieve a rough jammy texture. Remove and transfer to a small bowl.

Tip the cauliflower into a serving dish and squeeze over a little more lemon juice. Sprinkle over the sesame seeds and give it all a toss before serving. Serve the jam alongside it or spooned throughout the cauliflower.

Both the cauliflower and the jam will keep well for about 4-5 days in the fridge.

This recipe is foolproof: just one bunch of spring onions, a little olive oil and roughly one slice of lemon per person. An all-rounder, it's delicious with fish, meat or any vegetable dish. Despite its simplicity it is quite a showstopper and looks wonderful both in the tin and plated up – as pictured on page 158.

## Roasted spring onion salad with lemon

**Serves 4–6**

*4–6 bunches of spring onions, outer skins peeled and bottoms sliced off*

*1–2 lemons, finely sliced*

*olive oil, for drizzling*

*sea salt and black pepper*

Preheat the oven to 240°C/475°F/gas mark 9.

Place the spring onions and lemon slices on a roasting tray, drizzle with olive oil and season. Use your hands to coat the onions and rearrange the lemon so that it is evenly dispersed.

Roast for 20–25 minutes or until the onions are slightly charred and caramelised. Transfer to a serving plate and serve.

This is one of those recipes that is so easy it hardly needs writing down. It is a great way to make the humble carrot that bit more interesting and is wonderful with roast chicken. This speedy solution has often saved me on many Sunday lunches when I suddenly realise that it is ten to one and everything is ready except the carrots, which are still waiting patiently on the counter . . . I like my carrots with a bit of a kick, so I add cayenne pepper, but they taste quite delicious without it too. You could also use a pinch of ground nutmeg for more of a wintery, festive spice.

# Hokey smoked carrots

**Serves 4**

*4 large carrots, peeled and cut on a harsh diagonal, roughly 5cm wide*

*1 tbsp cold-pressed, extra-virgin olive oil*

*1 generous tbsp almond butter*

*½ tsp smoked paprika*

*pinch of cayenne pepper (optional)*

*sea salt and black pepper*

Boil or steam the carrots for about 5 minutes – you want them to have a bit of bite. Drain.

While still warm, combine them with the olive oil, almond butter, spices and salt and pepper. Stir well and transfer to a serving dish.

These three salads are perfect for those spontaneous gatherings. I am rarely daunted by suddenly having a few more mouths to feed as I always have at least a few of the below ingredients in my fridge to pull together into a quick salad. Paired with a good loaf or some leftover cold potatoes and a few soft-boiled eggs, they keep everyone happy. These salads are also great picnic fare – as well as being quick to make they travel with little fuss.

# Three foolproof five-minute salads

**Each salad serves 4**

## Carrot and grapefruit

*1 large pink grapefruit*

*3 tsp toasted sesame oil*

*3 tbsp cold-pressed olive oil*

*juice of ½ lemon*

*1 tbsp apple cider vinegar*

*6 medium–large carrots (about 350g), grated*

*6 tbsp black or white sesame seeds (optional)*

*sea salt and black pepper*

Zest the grapefruit into a large bowl then add the sesame oil, olive oil, lemon juice, vinegar and salt and pepper to taste. Whisk it all together with a fork.

Cutting the top and tail off the grapefruit so that you have a flat base, use a serrated knife to slice off the bitter white pith. Turn the grapefruit on its side and loosen the segments so that you are left with just the flesh and none of the skin.

Place the carrots and sesame seeds, if using, into the bowl with the dressing and toss until well combined before stirring through the grapefruit segments.

# Smashed cucumber and tahini

*1 large cucumber*

*2 tbsp tahini*

*2 tbsp cold-pressed olive oil*

*1 tbsp fresh lemon juice*

*pinch of sea salt*

*1 tsp nigella or sesame seeds (optional)*

Wash the cucumber and slice it in half lengthways. Run a teaspoon down the centre of the cucumber, remove the seeds and discard. Slice the cucumber into roughly finger-sized pieces and place in a freezer bag. If you don't have a freezer bag you can use cling film – double up two pieces, lie them out flat then place the cucumber on top and fold over the cling film.

Covering your wrapped cucumber with a tea towel, bash it with either a wooden spoon or rolling pin before transferring to a bowl. Try to retain as much water that may have been released as you can.

Mix the remaining ingredients, except the seeds, together in a small bowl and pour over the smashed cucumber. Scatter over the seeds, if using, and give everything a good stir.

# Avocado and yellow pepper smash

*2 ripe avocados, stoned*

*2 yellow or orange peppers, deseeded and finely sliced*

*zest and juice of 2 lemons or limes*

*sea salt and black pepper*

Scoop out the flesh of the avocados into a bowl and either using your hands or a fork smash it until you have a guacamole-like smoosh.

Add the sliced pepper and lime or lemon zest and juice, give everything a vigorous stir and smash with a fork. Season to taste and serve immediately to prevent the avocado browning.

I always feel sorry for the poor Brussels sprout. Hated by most children and just tolerated by many adults, they get most of their attention for being the brunt of Christmas jokes. My mission is to convince people of their splendid versatility. Roughly sliced and wokked with a little chilli, garlic and ginger, they are absolutely divine. This recipe is my favourite way to entice people onto the Brussels sprout wagon. Of course, you don't have to make the mayonnaise but it does make for a wonderful zingy dip and it takes no time at all.

## Share and tear tamari, miso-roasted Brussels sprout stalk *with zingy lime mayonnaise*

**Serves 6–8**

*1 Brussels sprout stalk (with sprouts attached)*

*4 tbsp coconut oil, softened*

*4 tbsp miso paste*

*2 tbsp tamari*

*2 tbsp mirin (optional)*

*juice of ½ lemon*

*1 garlic clove, crushed*

***For the mayonnaise***

*100ml rapeseed oil*

*100ml light olive oil*

*50ml sweet almond oil or walnut oil*

*5 tbsp fresh lime juice*

*1 tbsp mirin*

*1 tsp powdered mustard*

*2 egg yolks*

*pinch of salt*

To make the mayonnaise, first combine your oils and give them a stir. Then place the lime juice, mirin, powdered mustard and egg yolks in a food processor and combine until smooth. With the machine still on, add the combined oils in a thin stream and continue to process until you have a thick creamy consistency. Season with a little salt and allow it to rest.

Preheat the oven to 200°C/400°F/gas mark 6.

Wash the Brussels sprout stalk and pat it dry with a clean cloth. If it has a very long stalk you may want to trim it to fit into the oven or you could simply cut it in two and use two trays. Starting from the top and working your way down the stalk, first remove the tough outer leaves of each sprout head before lightly nicking the base of the stem of each in two places. This makes the sprouts easier to pull away once cooked.

In a small bowl, mix the remaining ingredients and then, using your hands, massage each of the sprout heads until they are all covered. Depending on the size of the stalk you may need to make a little more of the miso mix. Place the marinated stalk on the baking tray and roast in the oven for 45 minutes, rotating it about every 15 minutes to make sure it cooks evenly.

Once it is nicely browned and the Brussels sprout heads are cooked, remove from the oven and serve with the mayonnaise alongside, allowing people to pull off the sprout heads and dip into the mayonnaise.

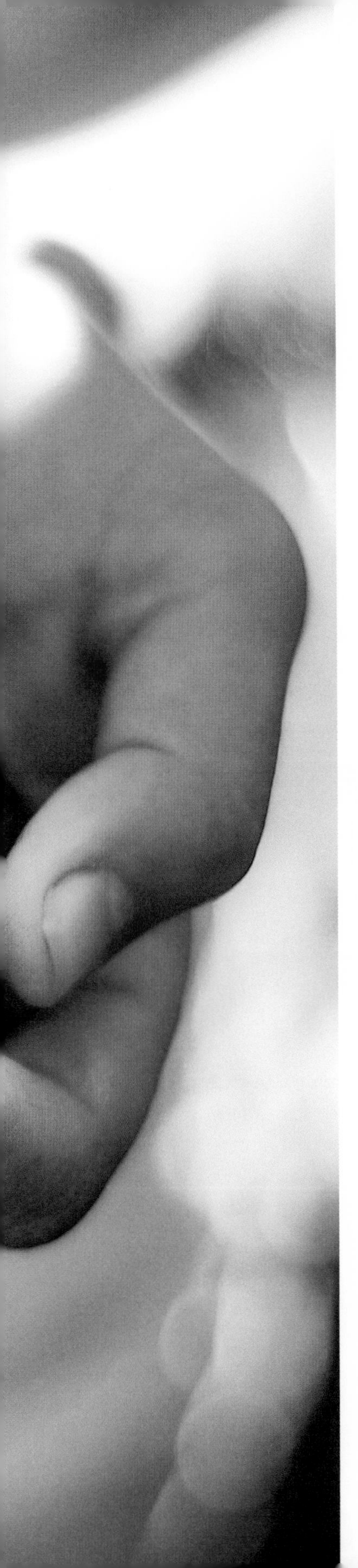

# Sweeter things

My grandmother always used to say that baking was good for the soul, and whenever she forecast a tantrum brewing she'd sweep me off to the kitchen to help her bake. I would calm right down, forgetting about whatever was bothering me and immersing myself in kneading, stirring, measuring and whisking. I still bake whenever I feel a little hot with stress and I believe it is one of the best cures. I have yet to find someone who truly doesn't enjoy a piece of cake or at least something sweet – even if just occasionally. There is nothing better than a mouthful of warm gooey brownie (see my Chocolate and hazelnut skillet brownie cake on page 190) or the sweet crisp edge of a cookie (Peanut butter and cacao nib cookies, page 198). I am never more popular at home or in the office than when I come bearing baked goods. Many of the recipes here also lend themselves brilliantly to being given as gifts, such as my Chilli, sea salt chocolate almonds (see page 204) and Chocolate toffee crunch (see page 202).

Nothing is better than the chewy, caramelised apple skin housing a sweet, soft, slow-cooked centre studded with treacly spiced pecans. Enjoyed with a scoop of real vanilla ice cream, tart Greek or coconut yoghurt, or even my sweet Cashew cream (page 231), this is hard to beat. My favourite way to enjoy this recipe is probably with a knob of my Espresso butter (page 236). The smooth coffee flavour seems to melt right through and the combination is utterly scrumptious.

# Baked apples

*with cinnamon toasted pecans*

**Serves 4**

*75g pecans*

*4 medium-sized Bramley (cooking) apples, core removed*

*5 tbsp maple syrup*

*½ tsp mixed spice*

*1 tbsp light brown soft sugar or coconut sugar*

***To serve, optional***

*Espresso butter (see page 236)*

*ice cream*

*Cashew cream (page 231)*

*Greek or coconut yoghurt*

Preheat the oven to 200°C/400°F/gas mark 6.

Place the pecans on a baking tray and toast them in the oven for about 10 minutes or until they have browned slightly and begun to smell fragrant. Make sure they don't burn. Remove and allow to cool slightly before roughly chopping.

Arrange the cored apples on another baking tray. To remove just the core of an apple you can invest in a fancy apple corer, but if you don't have one I find a sharp, thin knife works well too. Just make four slits around the stem, cutting a rough square, and fiddle a little with your knife to loosen the core completely before pushing it out. Next, slice 3 or 4 slits on the apple top to bottom; this helps them to cook.

In a small bowl, combine the cooled chopped nuts, syrup, mixed spice and sugar. Spoon the mix into the wells of the apples where their cores once were. Any extra nut mix that you cannot push in or that won't stay put on top can just be spooned onto the baking tray beside the apples. Bake for about 1 hour or until they are soft and their skins have browned nicely.

Serve with either a knob of the Espresso butter, a scoop of ice cream, Cashew cream or Greek or coconut yoghurt. If the Espresso butter is frozen, let it to come to room temperature while your apples are cooking.

A subtly spiced cake with thin slices of apple at both the top and bottom, I love this with a cup of strong, brewed tea. The spices are heavily influenced by my Dutch and German roots and it is a wonderful all-rounder that works both for elevenses and afternoon tea. I make this nearly all year round. I find Braeburn apples work best but a tart, firm apple such as a Granny Smith would work well too.

# Spiced apple tea cake

**Serves 12**

*225g butter, at room temperature, plus extra for greasing*

*300g light brown soft sugar or coconut sugar*

*1½ tbsp ground cinnamon*

*250g spelt flour (plain white or a gluten-free blend will work too)*

*1 tsp baking powder*

*1 tsp mixed spice*

*½ tsp salt*

*1 tsp vanilla extract*

*4 large eggs, at room temperature*

*6 large apples, peeled, cored and cut into 3mm slices*

*Greek yoghurt, to serve (optional)*

Preheat the oven to 180°C/350°F/gas mark 4 and grease and line a 23cm springform cake tin with baking parchment.

In a small bowl, combine 100g of the sugar with 1 tablespoon of the cinnamon.

In a second bowl, whisk together the flour, baking powder, remaining cinnamon, mixed spice and salt.

In a separate bowl, using an electric whisk, beat together the butter and remaining sugar until thick and smooth. Add the vanilla then the eggs, one at a time – you may need to scrape down the sides of the bowl once or twice. Pour in the flour mix and fold lightly to combine.

Combine the apples with three-quarters of the cinnamon/sugar mix. Add half the apples to the tin, making sure you cover the base. Pour the batter over the apples and smooth the edges, then arrange the remaining apples in a circular pattern on the top.

Sprinkle over the remaining cinnamon/sugar mix and bake for 1 hour. Cover loosely with foil, then bake for another 15 minutes or until the cake is set in the middle – a skewer inserted in the centre should come out clean.

Transfer the tin to a wire rack to cool slightly, then release the sides of the tin. Serve warm or at room temperature, either on its own or or with a spoonful of tart Greek yoghurt.

This deliciously moist cake is taken from a simple French recipe for yoghurt cake or Gâteau de Mamie, which translates as Granny Cake. My own version is made by dropping blueberries into the batter, which is what gives it the puddles. The berries tend to disperse in a random fashion within the cake when using thick or Greek yoghurt, and will usually sink all the way to the bottom if you use a plain, thinner yoghurt as it makes for a runnier batter. In this case I advise you invert the cake after baking as you would an upside-down cake. I use cold-pressed, extra virgin rapeseed oil over coconut oil here as its subtler flavour lends itself better to the cake, but you can use melted butter or coconut oil if you prefer.

# Yoghurt and lemon cake

*with blueberry puddles*

**Serves 10–12**

*175g light brown soft sugar or coconut sugar*

*3 large eggs*

*180g Greek or coconut yoghurt for evenly dispersed berries or plain yoghurt for a large puddle*

*120ml cold-pressed, extra virgin rapeseed oil (you can also use melted butter or coconut oil)*

*150g spelt flour (plain white, gluten-free blend works too)*

*1 tsp baking powder*

*½ tsp salt*

*zest of 2 lemons*

*150g punnet of blueberries, washed and patted dry*

**For the glaze**

*4 tbsp fresh lemon juice*

*4 tbsp honey*

Preheat the oven to 170°C/325°F/gas mark 3 and grease and line the base and sides of a 20cm round springform cake tin.

In a large bowl, whisk the sugar and eggs until slightly pale in colour. Stir in the yoghurt and oil until well blended.

In a separate bowl, whisk together the flour, baking powder, salt and zest. Tip the dry ingredients into the wet and fold in slowly until smooth.

Pour the batter into the prepared pan and sprinkle over the blueberries. Bake for 45 minutes, until the cake feels springy to the touch and a skewer inserted into the centre comes out clean with no crumbs.

Transfer the cake, in the tin, to a wire rack for about 15 minutes. Combine the lemon juice and honey in a small bowl and stir until smooth. Prick the cake a few times with a skewer and, using a teaspoon or pastry brush, gently paint the glaze all over the cake.

Leave to sit for 10 minutes before releasing the cake and transferring to a clean wire rack, allowing to cool completely. Depending on where your blueberries have settled, you may want to invert the cake.

The cake will keep for 4–5 days in an airtight container.

I first made skillet brownies when we were on a walking holiday in Scotland. Sitting round the campfire one evening, in the absence of marshmallows to toast, I decided to make something as equally gooey and delicious. I now often make this as a dinner party dessert and serve the brownie in all its chocolatey glory with some whipped cream, crème fraîche or my Honey, nut, Cointreau and tahini ice cream (page 216).

# Chocolate and hazelnut skillet brownie cake

**Serves 6**

*350g good-quality dark chocolate (75% cocoa solids), roughly chopped into marble-sized pieces*

*220g unsalted butter*

*2 large eggs*

*2 tsp vanilla extract*

*100g light brown soft sugar or coconut sugar*

*30g spelt flour (buckwheat works well too)*

*1 tsp gluten-free baking powder*

*pinch of salt*

*70g hazelnuts, toasted (see page 245) and roughly chopped*

*hand-whipped cream, crème fraîche or my no-churn ice cream (page 216), to serve (optional)*

Preheat the oven to 180°C/350°F/gas mark 4 and line a 30cm diameter skillet or cast-iron frying pan with baking parchment.

Combine 300g of the chocolate with the butter in a saucepan over a low heat, allowing the chocolate to melt slowly. Stir occasionally and remove once 90 per cent of the chocolate has melted. Leave the remaining chocolate to melt while the bowl is off the heat, then leave to cool for 10–15 minutes.

In a large bowl, whisk together the eggs, vanilla and sugar. Add the chocolate mixture to the egg mixture and whisk until combined.

In a separate bowl and using a clean whisk, whisk together the flour, baking powder and salt. Pour this into the chocolate mix along with the remaining 50g of chopped chocolate and most of your chopped hazelnuts (keeping some aside to sprinkle on top) and gently stir until just combined.

Pour the mixture into the skillet or frying pan. Sprinkle over your remaining hazelnuts and bake for 25–30 minutes, making sure you don't over-bake it. It should be cooked but still have a slight wobble in the middle.

Serve warm just as it is, or with some whipped cream, crème fraîche or my no churn ice cream.

This recipe has been a long-standing favourite in my house. It is wickedly rich and indulgent, which in my eyes is exactly how a cake should be. If sea salt isn't your thing, feel free to omit it – replacing it with espresso powder works brilliantly or you could just leave it straight chocolate. This cake makes for a wonderful coffee or tea-time treat.

## Sea-salted flourless chocolate torte

**Serves 12–14**

*225g butter, plus extra for greasing*

*60g light brown soft sugar or coconut sugar, plus a little extra for sprinkling*

*250g good-quality dark chocolate (70% cocoa solids)*

*5 eggs, at room temperature*

*2 tsp vanilla extract*

*1 heaped tsp good-quality sea salt, plus more for sprinkling (or 1 tsp instant espresso powder)*

*2 tbsp cacao or cocoa powder, for sprinkling (optional)*

*good cream, yoghurt or coconut yoghurt and a few sharp berries, to serve*

Preheat the oven to 160°C/325°F/gas mark 3 and lightly grease the base of a 22cm springform cake tin and line with baking parchment. Lightly grease the parchment, too, and sprinkle over a little sugar, shake the tin to evenly disperse and tip away the excess. Double-wrap the base and sides of the outside of the tin with tin foil, almost as though you are creating a second outer skin on the cake tin – you will be baking the torte in a bain marie, so you want to ensure no water gets into the cake during cooking.

Take a deep roasting tray in which your wrapped cake tin fits nicely. If the tin is touching the sides a little, do not fret.

Melt the chocolate and butter in a pan over a low heat, stirring frequently. Remove from the heat when most of the chocolate has melted and there are just a few small pieces left. These will continue to melt off the heat as the chocolate cools a little.

In a separate, medium bowl, whisk the eggs and sugar using an electric whisk for 2 minutes. Add the vanilla, sea salt and cacao/cocoa and whisk again to combine. Gradually pour in the melted chocolate, changing the whisk speed to the slowest setting.

Pour the mix into the tin and give the base of the tin a few flicks with your index finger to remove any air bubbles. I find placing it on a flat surface and giving it a little bit of a wobble also helps.

cont.

Fill a kettle with water and boil. Place the tin into the roasting tray and slide the tray onto the middle rack of the oven. Pull out the rack as much as you can without putting the cake into slipping danger and slowly pour in the boiling water from the kettle until it comes to about 2cm up the side of the tin. Bake for 45–50 minutes or until the cake has set but the centre still looks soft.

Carefully remove from the oven, making sure you don't splash any water into the cake, then slowly draw the tin out of the water and place on a flat surface lined with a tea towel. Peel the foil away from the tin, again taking care as there may be a few leaks which will be very hot, then place the cake in the tin on a wire rack to cool completely.

To serve, release the sides of the tin and invert onto a plate. Dust the cake with some cacao or cocoa powder and sprinkle with a pinch of salt – sprinkle from a good height to get a nice even fall of salt. I like to serve this with some good cream or yoghurt and a few berries on the side. I love the sharpness of redcurrants, but for a sweeter option, strawberries or raspberries work too.

I like to think of these as my grown-up cookies. Rich, chocolatey and not overly sweet, they have the perfect balance of crispiness and chew. The espresso hit is strong, so use good-quality coffee – it makes all the difference. As this recipe makes quite a few cookies I sometimes freeze half of my cookie dough. The best way to do this is to roll the dough into balls and place these on a parchment lined tray in the freezer until frozen. You can then transfer them to a freezer bag and pull a few out whenever the urge for a cookie strikes. I would recommend allowing the frozen dough to thaw for about 20 minutes before baking.

# Espresso cookies

**Makes about 34 small cookies**

*350g good-quality dark chocolate (70% cocoa solids)*

*250g spelt flour (plain white or gluten-free blend works too)*

*80g Dutch-processed cocoa powder or cacao powder*

*1 tsp bicarbonate of soda*

*½ tsp sea salt*

*4 tbsp fresh finely ground coffee*

*250g butter, softened, or coconut oil*

*220g light brown soft sugar or coconut sugar*

*2 large eggs, at room temperature*

*1 tsp vanilla extract*

Preheat the oven to 180°C/350°F/gas mark 4. Line two baking sheets with baking parchment.

Chop the chocolate into roughly 5mm pieces – don't worry about little shards and any very small flakes, these will melt deliciously into the cookies.

In a medium bowl, whisk together the flour, cocoa powder, bicarbonate of soda, sea salt and ground coffee. Set aside.

In a separate, large bowl, using an electric whisk, beat the butter or coconut oil and sugar until light and fluffy. If you are using coconut oil, beat it until just incorporated, otherwise you will melt the oil. Beat in the eggs one by one, followed by the vanilla.

Pour the flour mix into the wet mix and gently fold in, adding the chopped chocolate halfway through. If your dough is very wet, transfer it to the fridge for 20 mins to firm up.

Roll the cookie dough using your hands into roughly golf-ball-sized balls and line them up on the baking sheets with at least 3cm between them.

Bake the cookies in the oven for about 10 minutes or until the edges are firm but the centres are just soft. Remove and leave them to cool on the baking sheets for 10 minutes, then transfer to a wire rack to cool completely. Store in an airtight container for up to 1 week.

Peanut butter cookies were one of my childhood weekend staple bakes. My mother would bake them with my sister and me, using the best peanut butter, that we would bring back by the suitcase-load from trips to Amsterdam. This recipe is a grown-up take on the peanut butter cookie. I like to use coconut sugar, which adds a caramel note, and the addition of cacao nibs gives these an exciting texture. You could also use chopped chocolate in the place of the nibs, which would be equally delicious.

# Peanut butter and cacao nib cookies

**Makes roughly 18 cookies**

*125g unsalted butter, at room temperature, or 100g coconut oil, soft but not melted*

*120g coconut sugar (light brown soft sugar will work too)*

*140g good-quality crunchy peanut butter*

*1 large egg*

*1 tsp vanilla extract*

*175g spelt or wholegrain flour (plain white or a gluten-free blend will work too)*

*1 tsp bicarbonate of soda*

*50g cacao nibs*

Preheat the oven to 170°C/350°F/gas mark 4 and line two baking sheets with baking parchment.

In a large bowl, cream the butter or oil and sugar together until it is pale and fluffy. Beat in the peanut butter until smooth, then add the egg and vanilla and beat again.

In a separate bowl, whisk together the flour and bicarbonate of soda. Stir in the cacao nibs.

Pour the dry mixture into the wet mixture and fold until everything comes together to form a sticky cookie batter.

Using 2 teaspoons, drop roughly golf-ball-sized amounts of cookie batter onto the baking sheets, making sure there is at least 3cm between each cookie. Bake for 10–12 minutes or until the cookies are nicely brown and their edges have begun to crisp. The centres should still be a little soft. Leave to cool on the baking sheets for about 10 minutes, then transfer to a wire rack and leave to cool completely.

Store in an airtight container – they should keep for up to 1 week.

There is a wonderful little patisserie right in the heart of Soho called Maison Bertaux. Often I go there to collect my thoughts in a journal and do a little people-watching. I will order a pot of loose-leaf tea and always treat myself to one of their traditional macaroons. These biscuits remind me of their fabulous macaroons, for they have a similar rustic look and chewiness. The taste is similar to a meringue but with a, denser and nuttier texture. They make wonderful gifts for friends, too, and will store very well if kept in an airtight container.

# Rustic macaroon biscuits

**Makes roughly 30 small cookies**

*175g light brown soft sugar or coconut sugar*

*200g skin-on, whole almonds, toasted (see page 245)*

*zest of 2 oranges*

*zest of 1 lemon*

*½ tsp vanilla powder*

*¼ tsp ground cloves*

*pinch of salt*

*3 large egg whites*

Preheat the oven to 150°C/300°F/gas mark 2 and line 2 baking sheets with baking parchment.

Tip the sugar into the bowl of a food processor and pulse for a few minutes just to create a finer texture. Remove about 3 tablespoons and set aside.

Add the almonds to the processor and pulse a few times, then pulse continuously until the almonds have broken down to a flour.

Transfer this to a large bowl and add the orange and lemon zest, vanilla powder, cloves and salt and whisk to combine.

In a separate bowl using an electric hand-held whisk, beat the egg whites until foamy before slowly adding the reserved sugar, ½ tablespoon at a time. Increase the beater speed and beat until you have a glossy mix and the sugar has dissolved. Fold into the almond mix until just blended.

Use 2 spoons to transfer heaped teaspoons of the mix onto the baking sheets, making sure to leave at least 4cm between each. Bake for 20–25 minutes or until they are slightly puffed and beginning to brown at the edges. You may want to rotate the sheets halfway through cooking to ensure an even bake.

Transfer the biscuits, still on the baking sheets, to a wire rack and leave to cool completely before removing.

A little reminiscent of the much-loved childhood favourite, the Daim bar, this is crunchy, chewy and wonderfully sweet. Make sure you let the toffee cool completely before adding the chocolate.

# Chocolate toffee crunch

**Makes about 20 bite-sized pieces**

*100g toasted hazelnuts (see page 245)*

*150g butter*

*150g light brown soft sugar or coconut sugar*

*2 tbsp honey or maple syrup*

*200g good-quality dark chocolate (70% cocoa solids)*

Line a 20 × 30cm baking tin with baking parchment.

In a food processor, blitz the toasted hazelnuts until they resemble a flour.

In a heavy-bottomed saucepan, melt the butter, sugar and honey or maple syrup over a medium–high heat and stir until the sugar is dissolved. Bring the mixture to the boil until it starts to bubble up the pan – this takes about 9 minutes, you'll know it's ready when it smells like caramel. Be careful not to let it burn.

Remove the pan from the heat and add the hazelnut flour, and stir until it's well incorporated. Put back on the heat and stir for another minute.

Pour the mixture into the tin and spread out the caramel mix with a spatula, making sure to work fast before it sets. Leave to cool and set in the fridge for 1 hour.

Break the chocolate into a heatproof bowl and melt it slowly by placing the bowl over a saucepan of simmering water, making sure the base of the bowl is not touching the water. Spread the melted chocolate over the set caramel and put the tin in the fridge for another hour.

Break the slab into small bite-sized pieces and enjoy as they are, or bag up into little cellophane bags to make gifts for your loved ones.

Dainty and delicate with a subtle chilli kick, with these you can go as spicy and as salty as you like with these. If chilli isn't to your liking, you can either leave out or swap it for some ground ginger or cinnamon. These make for wonderful gifts. Just wrap them in cellophane (I often ask for extra when buying flowers) and tie with string or ribbon.

# Chilli, sea salt chocolate almonds

**Makes a medium-sized bowl or approx. 6 gift bags**

*300g whole, skin-on almonds*

*1–2 tsp cayenne pepper (depending on how much heat you would like)*

*½ tsp coarse sea salt, plus extra for sprinkling (optional)*

*1 tbsp coconut oil or butter*

*120g good-quality dark chocolate (70% cocoa solids)*

Preheat the oven to 180°C/350°F/gas mark 4.

Place the almonds in a bowl with the cayenne pepper and sea salt. Melt the coconut oil or butter and pour it over the nuts. Stir until all the almonds are covered, then spread them out on a baking tray and placing in the oven for about 15 minutes or until they begin to smell fragrant. Be careful not to burn them.

Remove from the oven and leave to cool. Line a separate baking tray with baking parchment or greaseproof paper.

Once the almonds are cool, break the chocolate into a heatproof bowl and melt it slowly by placing the bowl over a saucepan of simmering water, making sure the base of the bowl is not touching the water. Once the chocolate has melted, remove it from the pan.

Transfer the almonds to the bowl of chocolate and stir to coat. Transfer them to the lined baking tray using a fork. Leave space between each almond so that the chocolate does not merge. You can sprinkle flecks of sea salt onto each almond once they are coated in chocolate, if you like. If you are doing this, allow them to harden at room temperature as opposed to the fridge, and add the salt after about 5 minutes when the chocolate is a little cooler – so as not to melt the salt.

Store the chocolate-coated almonds in a glass jar or little cellophane bags if you are making them for gifts. They should keep for a good 5 weeks at room temperature and up to 2 months in the fridge.

A hybrid between sweet and savoury, these biscuits have a real kick to them that is similar to a ginger biscuit but with a little more punch. Closer to a cookie than a gingersnap in texture, they have a crisp outside and soft centre. Fresh rosemary is essential for these. If you are not a huge fan of spice, try using mild chilli powder instead of cayenne pepper. The kick is held back whilst the flavour is still interesting. You don't have to use the best-quality olive oil here but I do find a good oil adds a more exciting pepperiness to the biscuit.

## Rosemary, cayenne and olive oil biscuits

**Makes about 20**

*200g spelt or wholegrain flour*

*100g light brown soft sugar or coconut sugar*

*1 tsp baking powder*

*½ tsp bicarbonate of soda*

*¼ tsp sea salt*

*¼ tsp cayenne pepper*

*2 tsp black pepper*

*2 tbsp freshly chopped rosemary*

*75ml cold-pressed, extra-virgin olive oil*

*1 large egg*

*juice of ½ lemon*

Preheat the oven to 180°C/350°F/gas mark 4 and line two baking sheets with baking parchment.

In a large bowl, whisk together the flour, sugar, baking powder, bicarbonate of soda, salt, cayenne pepper and freshly ground black pepper. Stir in the chopped rosemary.

In a separate, small bowl or measuring jug, whisk together the oil, egg and lemon juice.

Pour the wet ingredients into the dry and bring everything together using a wooden spoon or spatula.

Roll the dough into small balls (just a bit smaller than a golf ball). Slightly pat the biscuits down either on the tray or still in your hands. Arrange the biscuits about 2cm away from each other on the tray and bake for 10–12 minutes. The tops should be crisp to the touch.

Allow the biscuits to cool for about 5 minutes on the tray before transferring them to a wire rack to cool completely.

They will keep for up to 5 days in an airtight container.

One of my ultimate treats as a child was peanut brittle. I used to seek it out like a magpie at country fairs and trips to Brighton Pier – and still do. I was immensely proud when I first made this and despite it most definitely being a sweet treat I do feel it is slightly more grown-up with the addition of pumpkin seeds. I usually have a batch in the cupboard to sprinkle over homemade ice creams or to give my yoghurt a little crunch. The brittle makes a great gift wrapped in cellophane – you can buy cellophane online but I often ask for a few extra sheets from my local flower stand when I am picking up a bunch of flowers.

# Pumpkin seed brittle

**Makes 1 tray of brittle**

*70g unsalted butter*

*120g light brown soft sugar or coconut sugar*

*4 tbsp wild flower honey*

*pinch of vanilla powder*

*130g pumpkin seeds, toasted and cooled (see page 245)*

Line a baking sheet with baking parchment and grease well.

Melt the butter in a large saucepan set over a medium heat then add the sugar and honey. Stir to combine and watch it carefully to make sure it doesn't burn.

The mixture should start to bubble quite a bit before it rises up the sides of the pan. This usually takes about 5 minutes. Once this has started to happen, let it bubble for about another minute – it should smell of caramel and have darkened in colour and be bubbling vigorously.

Taking care not to splash yourself (the caramel will be very hot), sprinkle in the vanilla powder, pour in the pumpkin seeds and give everything a stir.

Pour onto the baking sheet and use a greased spatula to flatten – work quickly, as it will cool very rapidly.

Allow the brittle to fully cool before peeling it off the parchment and breaking into pieces.

Store in an airtight container, where it will keep for up to 5 weeks.

One of my most precious memories is the summer my parents rented an old château in France. The house had an orchard and often the grass beneath the trees was dotted with fallen plums and greengages. We used to run around in the grass dodging what we called the 'ugly fruit' niftily with our bare feet. It was here with all the 'ugly fruit' that I first made my 'ugly fruit tart'. I make this any time I find some forgotten fruit in the fruit bowl as it is a beautiful way to salvage any cosmetically challenged produce that would otherwise be shunned. Apricots, apples, peaches, nectarines and plums work very well here, as do figs.

# Ugly fruit tart

**Serves 8–10**

***For the pastry***

*200g spelt flour (plain white, a gluten-free blend or buckwheat will work too), plus extra for dusting*

*½ tsp ground cinnamon*

*½ tsp fine sea salt*

*100g unsalted butter or coconut oil, chilled and cut into pieces*

*70g of your favourite nuts (I like a mix of hazelnuts and almonds), toasted and blitzed in a food processor to a slightly coarse flour*

*1 large egg*

*3 tbsp ice-cold water*

*1 egg yolk, lightly beaten or 2 tbsp nut milk*

***For the filling***

*6 ripe plums, stoned and cut into slices*

*cont.*

First make the pastry. I like to use a food processor to do this as it is quicker, but if you have cold hands you can use your fingers, too. Pulse the flour, cinnamon and salt in the food processor to combine. Add the chilled and cubed butter or oil as well as a generous handful of the coarse nut flour (keep the rest for later). Pulse again until you have what resembles coarse breadcrumbs and the large chunks of butter have broken down.

Add the egg and 3 tablespoons of water and pulse until you have a dough. Remove the dough from the bowl of the food processor and shape it into a thick disc. Wrap in cling film and place it in the fridge to chill for at least half an hour.

When you are ready to bake the tart, preheat the oven to 180°C/350°F/gas mark 4 and line a flat baking tray with baking parchment.

Toss the fruit, sugar, cornflour, ginger, cinnamon, if using, and vanilla together in a large bowl.

Lightly flour a work surface before rolling out your pastry to a rough circle shape about 35cm in diameter. Transfer the rolled pastry onto your lined sheet. I find the easiest way to do this is to use your rolling pin to gently roll the flattened pastry back over the pin before lifting it and rolling it back over the lined baking sheet.

cont.

*4 ripe figs, quartered or sliced*

*1–2 tbsp light brown soft sugar or coconut sugar, plus 1 tbsp for sprinkling*

*1 tsp cornflour/arrowroot*

*1 tsp ground ginger*

*1 tsp ground cinnamon (optional)*

*2 tsp pure vanilla extract*

**To serve**

*crème fraîche, Cashew cream (see page 231), Ice cream (page 216), to serve*

Sprinkle the reserved nut flour in a circle over the pastry, leaving a 4cm border. Pour over your fruit and arrange to make sure the nut flour is covered. Then, using your fingers, gently work your way around the tart, rolling the pastry up around the fruit. It's quite alright for this to be a messy job and will only make the tart look more rustic.

Brush the beaten egg yolk or nut milk over the pastry using a pastry brush and sprinkle over a little sugar, if you wish.

Bake for 30–35 minutes or until the pastry is golden. Enjoy warm or at room temperature with crème fraîche, ice cream (page 216), Cashew cream (page 231) or a spoonful of yoghurt.

It's a yearly ritual in my family to go blackberry picking. A picnic is packed and we each bring a basket to fill to the brim. Many are eaten along the way, the very ripe ones are reserved for jam but a good proportion are always kept for my little galettes. Delicate pastry hugs the sweet fruit and bursts of berry juice explode over the edge – don't be distressed by these berry bursts or pastry cracks, these are the best bit! I often like to use blueberries to make these galettes, too, or you could use a mix of both.

# Wild berry, hazelnut and pecan galettes

**Makes 8 galettes**

***For the filling***

*600g blackberries (blueberries will work too)*

*2 tbsp cornflour*

*2 tsp lemon juice*

*1½ tsp vanilla extract*

*80g light brown soft sugar or coconut sugar, plus 1 tbsp for sprinkling*

*fresh cream, yoghurt and a few mint leaves, to serve*

***For the pastry***

*30g pecan nuts*

*30g hazelnuts*

*200g spelt flour (plain or buckwheat works too), plus extra for dusting*

*1 tsp ground cinnamon*

*½ tsp fine sea salt*

*cont.*

Preheat the oven to 180°C/350°F/gas mark 4.

Spread the pecans and hazelnuts over a baking sheet and toast in the oven, tossing halfway through, for 10–12 minutes or until they are beginning to smell fragrant. Allow the nuts to cool, then place them in a food processor and pulse until you have a coarse, flour-like texture. Transfer to a bowl.

Add the spelt flour or alternative, cinnamon and salt to the blender and pulse to combine. Add the butter or oil, pulse, then add a small handful of the nut flour, then pulse until the mixture is crumble-like – do not over-pulse or you will melt the butter.

Add the egg and ice-cold water and pulse until you have a dough. Remove the dough from the bowl of the food processor and shape it into a thick disc. Wrap in cling film and place it in the fridge to chill for at least half an hour.

When you are ready to bake the galettes, preheat the oven to 180°C/350°F/gas mark 4 and line a flat baking tray with baking parchment.

Toss the berries, cornflour, lemon juice, vanilla extract and sugar in a bowl.

Divide each of the pastry discs into four. On a lightly floured surface, roll out the first four pastry discs. Using half of your reserved nut flour, sprinkle equal amounts over the centre of each disc, leaving about a 2cm border.

cont.

*100g unsalted butter or coconut oil, chilled and cut into pieces*

*1 large egg*

*3 tbsp ice-cold water*

*1 egg yolk, lightly beaten, or 3 tbsp nut milk*

Divide the berries among the galettes, leaving a 2cm border. Gently fold over the pastry to encase the berries. Don't worry if the pastry breaks slightly, just patch any holes up by squeezing the edges together with your fingers, or patching with any excess pastry.

Carefully slide the galettes onto the baking sheet lined with baking parchment and repeat the process using your second pastry disc until you have 8 berry galettes on two baking sheets.

Brush the pastry with a little beaten egg yolk or nut milk and sprinkle with a little sugar. Bake for 30–35 minutes or until the pastry is golden brown.

Enjoy with fresh cream or a spoonful of yoghurt. I love to tear over a few mint leaves too.

Gelato is my ultimate treat and something I treat myself to often. The best, of course, is found in Rome, but there is something incredibly satisfying about making your own ice cream, and when I have the time there are two variations I love to make. At the risk of catastrophically failing to create anything near as good as the true original I take a different approach that requires no ice cream churner. I had one once when I was eighteen but I found the darn thing so bulky I had to get rid of it. These recipes suit me well and I often make slight variations to them too. Almond butter is delicious in place of tahini in this one, as is the addition of grated chocolate.

# Honey, nut, Cointreau and tahini ice cream

**Makes 1 x 900g loaf tin**

*60g clear honey*

*40g tahini*

*1 tsp vanilla extract*

*4 tbsp Cointreau*

*4 eggs*

*100g golden caster sugar*

*300ml double cream*

*50g shelled pistachios, roughly chopped*

*50g toasted almonds, roughly chopped (see page 244)*

Wash and dry a 900g loaf tin or similar shaped dish. Medium size Pyrex dishes work well too.

In a small bowl, mix together the honey, tahini, vanilla extract and Cointreau and set aside.

Separate the eggs, placing the egg whites in a large bowl and the yolks in a smaller bowl. Lightly whisk together the egg yolks.

Using an electric hand whisk, whisk the egg whites until you can see stiff peaks. Slowly add the caster sugar and continue to whisk until the egg whites are stiff and glossy.

In a separate bowl, whisk the cream until soft peaks form.

Fold the egg yolks into the cream then add the cream mix and half the honeyed tahini to the egg whites. Fold in, then add the remaining honeyed tahini as well as the nuts. Do not over-mix.

Pour the ice cream into your lined loaf tin. Lightly cover the ice cream with a sheet of baking parchment then wrap the loaf tin in cling film and freeze for at least 2–3 hours.

Before serving, remove the ice cream from the freezer for 5 minutes just to soften it a little. This makes it the perfect consistency.

This dark chocolate sorbet is one of my greatest pleasures. The taste is rich and pure. I enjoy this just as it is, served with a few sharp berries, but it also delicious with a pinch of cayenne pepper or nutmeg for a little warm kick. The vodka helps with the texture and is a useful addition here, but if you'd prefer an alcohol-free version, feel free to leave it out.

# Dark chocolate sorbet

**Makes roughly 500ml**

*80g Dutch-processed cocoa*

*150g golden caster sugar*

*50g light brown soft sugar or coconut sugar*

*½ tsp cayenne pepper or nutmeg (optional)*

*160g good-quality dark chocolate (no less than 80%), chopped*

*1 tsp vanilla extract*

*pinch of salt*

*1 tbsp vodka (optional)*

Begin by placing a freezer-safe, wide bowl in the freezer – a metal one is even better.

Allow it to get really cold before starting on your sorbet.

Place the cocoa, sugars and spices, if using, and 600ml of water in a large saucepan and bring it to the boil, whisking it frequently. Allow it to boil for about a minute, keeping an eye on it and continuing to whisk.

Remove from the heat and stir in the chocolate, vanilla and salt until the mix is smooth and there are no lumps. Transfer to your chilled bowl and continue to whisk for another minute or so before covering with cling film and placing in the freezer.

After about 1 hour or when the sorbet has frozen about 3cm from the edges, add the vodka (this helps to prevent ice crystals) and whisk it again. Return to the freezer for another hour before whisking it again.

You may want to whisk and freeze for a third time, but it is not essential. At this point you can transfer the sorbet to a more convenient-shaped Tupperware or tub before allowing it to completely freeze. I usually just leave mine in the bowl.

Before serving, remove the sorbet from the freezer for 10 minutes just to soften it a little. This makes it the perfect consistency.

Creamy, rich and with a nutty crunch, these coconut truffles are one of my favourite things to make. The rum and coconut gives them a bit of a boozy, tropical twist and they are rather fun to end a dinner party with. You can be versatile with your flavouring but I love infusing them with alcohol. If you prefer your truffles alcohol-free you can omit the rum and instead add a subtle hint of lemon zest or cinnamon and ginger. These truffles are best enjoyed chilled, so I like to keep them in the fridge until ready to serve.

## Hazelnut, rum and coconut truffles

**Makes about 30 truffles**

*300g good-quality dark chocolate, very finely chopped (80% cocoa solids)*

*250ml full-fat coconut milk from a tin, well-stirred*

*1 tbsp maple syrup or honey (optional)*

***For the coating***

*About 60g hazelnuts (or use cocoa powder or desiccated coconut)*

***For the flavourings***

*1–2 tbsp rum or brandy*

*1 tsp very finely grated lemon zest*

*¼ tsp ground cinnamon and ground ginger*

Preheat the oven to 180°C/350°F/gas mark 4.

First prepare the hazelnuts, if using. Tip the nuts on a baking tray and roast in the oven for 10–12 minutes or until they begin to smell fragrant and their skins split slightly. Be careful not to burn them. Allow the nuts to cool, then lay them out on a tea towel. Roughly fold or scrunch the tea towel over the nuts and, using your hands, give them a good rub to brush off their skins. Blitz the nuts in a food processor to a coarse flour and set aside for later.

Place the chopped chocolate into a medium heatproof or glass bowl. Have a saucepan lid or plate ready to act as a lid later on. Bring the coconut milk to a simmer in a small saucepan over a low–medium heat. Pour this over the chocolate and immediately cover the bowl with the lid or plate to keep the heat in. After 5 minutes, remove the lid, add the rum or brandy and stir gently.

Once smooth, place the mix in the fridge, uncovered, for 2–3 hours or until set but still pliable.

Spread your hazlenut flour or preferred coating on a small plate. Using a teaspoon and your fingers, gently roll the truffles into even little balls, then roll them in the chopped hazelnuts, cocoa or coconut.

Set the truffles on a dish or tray lined with baking parchment and return to the fridge for a further 3 hours or overnight. Leave the truffles in the fridge and remove just before serving, They will keep in the fridge for up to 3 weeks.

# A little extra

There are a handful of things that I have found make life that bit easier and that bit more delicious. A well-stocked spice cupboard and good-quality olive oil are essential elements, but I have a few more ingredients that, although less conventional, have become staples of my kitchen. These can be added to dishes to give them a little more flair or kept in jam jars and picked on when one's tummy begins to rumble and it's a little too early for supper. Although incredibly simple, these little gems can make all the difference.

I must confess that whenever I make granola usually less than half of it sees the depths of a breakfast bowl. For the most part I enjoy snacking on it in handfuls from the jar, or using it as a topping for yoghurt, porridge, soups, salads or stir-fries. This savoury granola is perfect for this kind of topping and snacking way of eating. It also makes for a very good travel snack packed in a small sealable container.

## Savoury oat and buckwheat granola

**Makes 1 medium jar**

*100g jumbo oats*

*70g raw buckwheat groats*

*40g flaked almonds (untoasted)*

*40g pumpkin seeds*

*40g sunflower seeds*

*60g almonds, roughly chopped*

*2 lemongrass stalks, outer leaves removed and finely chopped*

*2 tbsp lemon juice*

*4 tbsp coconut oil, melted*

*3 tbsp tamari*

*1½ tbsp maple syrup*

*½ tsp turmeric*

*½ tsp cayenne pepper*

*½ tsp ground ginger*

*good pinch of sea salt*

*good grind of freshly ground black pepper*

*handful of flaked coconut*

Preheat the oven to 160°C/325°F/gas mark 3 and line a large baking tray with baking parchment.

Combine all the ingredients apart from the flaked coconut in a large bowl and stir to combine. Spread everything onto the tray and bake in the oven for 20 minutes, tossing halfway. About 5 minutes from the end of the cooking time, stir through the coconut. The granola should be crisp and dry when cooked. Allow it to cool completely before storing in an airtight container for up to 5 weeks.

I adore pesto but I do find that pine nuts can be incredibly expensive. With a hefty pesto habit and generally having an abundant supply of sunflower seeds at home, I set about experimenting with less costly options. The result is delicious. I love using basil, parsley, coriander and tarragon but I recommend playing around with a variety of your favourite herbs. Stir into pasta, spread onto toast or spoon over potatoes, chicken or fish.

# Poor man's pesto

**Makes 1 large jar of pesto**

*3 large handfuls of herbs – basil, coriander or parsley, roughly chopped with the stems chopped a little finer*

*4 tbsp tarragon leaves, chopped (optional)*

*100g sunflower seeds, toasted (see page 244)*

*1–2 garlic cloves, crushed (depending on how much garlic you like)*

*about 150ml or more cold-pressed, extra-virgin olive oil*

*juice of 1 lemon (or more)*

*sea salt*

Combine the herbs, sunflower seeds and garlic in a food processor and pulse until broken down. You can make the pesto as fine as you wish. I prefer mine a little chunky.

Slowly add the olive oil and lemon juice with the motor still running until you reach the consistency you desire. Season with salt to taste. Transfer to sterilised jars (see page 228) or an airtight container.

This will keep for about a week in the fridge.

Sauerkraut has become rather a fashionable food in recent years but it's something that I grew up with, having Dutch and German grandparents. Generally we ate the classics like straight cabbage sauerkraut, but there is something about the depth of flavour in this recipe that I love. It almost has a sweetness to it that goes wonderfully well with practically anything. You can go a little lighter on the spices for a milder taste but the intensity does mellow out over time, too, so don't worry if it's rather kapow at first.

# Persian-spiced sauerkraut

**Makes 1 x 2.5-litre jar**

*1 head of green pointed cabbage, sliced into varying thicknesses for texture*

*1 heaped tbsp salt, plus 1 tbsp extra (optional)*

*1 tsp coriander seeds*

*½ tsp fennel seeds*

*seeds from within 6 cardamom pods*

*½ tsp cumin seeds*

*1 tsp ground ginger*

*1 tsp ground cinnamon*

*½ tsp sweet smoked paprika*

*½ tsp nutmeg (or 1 tsp mixed spice)*

Place the cabbage in a large bowl and toss it in the salt. Set aside to rest for 1 hour or until it starts to sweat.

Place the spices in a pestle and mortar and crush them before adding to the cabbage and tossing to combine. If you don't have a pestle and mortar just use a sturdy bowl and either the end of a rolling pin or the lid of a small spice jar to bash them with.

Transfer everything, including any liquid that may have formed, into a sterilised jar (see below). Using clean hands, punch the cabbage down hard. As you do this you'll notice more liquid releasing from the cabbage. After you've pushed it down as much as you can, place something heavy on top of the cabbage to continue to push it down. I usually use another jam jar (sterilised) filled with water or rice.

Cover the jar with a dry cloth and secure it with either a rubber band or string. Return to it every few hours to punch the cabbage down again further, replacing the weighted jar each time as you do. The aim is to get the cabbage completely submerged within its own juices. If after 24 hours the cabbage is still not covered, dissolve 1 tablespoon of salt in about 200ml of water and add as much as you need to fully submerge the cabbage.

cont.

Keep the jar covered with the cloth and place it in a cool dark place. Check it daily, pushing down any cabbage that has begun to float above the liquid. Leave it for anywhere between 3 and 6 days – it is up to you how fermented you like it. Begin tasting after three days.

If you see any white bubbles or froth, don't panic. This is part of the fermenting process and can be skimmed off the top either whilst it is fermenting or just before you put it in the fridge. If you see any green mould, though, you may need to discard your kraut and start again.

I like to divide my sauerkraut into smaller sterilised jars and keep them in the fridge. Unopened sauerkraut can keep for up to 3 months.

How to sterilise jars: preheat the oven to 140°C/275°F/gas mark 1 and wash the jars and their lids in hot, soapy water. Rinse well and place them on a baking sheet and set in the oven to dry completely. If you are using jars with rubber ring seals, remove these before placing the jars in the oven as the heat will damage them. Instead, leave them in some freshly boiled water for 5 minutes or so.

I call this a salad but it is more of a hybrid between a salsa and tabbouleh. The herb-nut ratio to salad leaf is high here and the flavour is not for the faint-hearted. It is a very good accompaniment to fish or meat, or even on the side of an omelette, and a heaped tablespoon per person is usually enough. You can buy flaked almonds ready toasted to speed things up, but if you can't find them you can easily toast them at home (see page 244).

# Toasted almond, rocket and parsley salad

**Serves 4**

*½ bag of rocket*

*1 bunch of flat leaf parsley, leaves only*

*½ tsp coriander seed, crushed*

*4 tbsp cold-pressed, extra-virgin olive oil*

*2 tbsp red wine vinegar*

*1 tbsp pomegranate molasses or honey*

*120g flaked almonds (preferably toasted, see page 244)*

*sea salt and black pepper*

Place the rocket and parsley leaves in a food processor and pulse until roughly broken down. Scrape out into a large bowl.

Crush your coriander seed using a pestle and mortar. Alternatively, you can place them in a small bowl and use the back end of a rolling pin or even the spice jar itself to crush them.

In a small bowl, combine the crushed coriander seed, oil, vinegar and pomegranate molasses or honey. Season to taste and pour over the mushed salad, then scatter in the almonds. Toss well, taste and add extra seasoning, if needed. If the rocket is particularly strong you may wish to add a little more sweetness.

This salad is best eaten straight away when it is good and crunchy, but you can eat it a few days on – it will keep for about 5 days in an airtight container in the fridge. You can also stir it into pasta along with some olive oil.

One of my favourite things about making juice is the pulpy crackers you can make from all the leftover juicy bits that collect at the back of the machine. If you don't have a juicer you can also use a food processor to get some veggie pulp. I give two options to make here: one for more of a flatbread and the other for a dried-out cracker. If you are taking the flatbread route be sure to eat these within two days and keep them in the fridge to keep them fresh. I usually pop them in the toaster or under the grill for a quick warm-up just before eating.

## Veggie pulp flatbreads and crackers

**Makes 8 flat breads or crackers**

*250g veggie juice pulp (carrot works best)*

*150g milled flaxseed*

*2 tsp ground coriander*

*1 tsp ground cumin*

*1 tsp mild chilli powder*

*heaped tsp salt*

*good grind of pepper*

*1 large egg*

*75–100ml water*

Preheat the oven to 160°C/325°F/gas mark 3 and line a flat baking tray with baking parchment.

Combine the veggie pulp, flaxseed, spices, salt, pepper, egg and water in a bowl until well blended. You want to have a sticky, wet, spreadable mix but don't want it to be too watery.

Spread the mix over the baking tray, flattening it with a spatula or the back of a damp spoon. Using a table knife score into 8 flatbread shapes; four times across horizontally and once down the middle vertically.

For a softer flatbread bake for about 40 minutes before using a spatula to rotate the crackers and bake for a further 20 minutes.

For a fully dried-out cracker bake as above before reducing the oven to its lowest setting and continue to cook the crackers for a further 30–40 minutes or until completely dried out, turning every so often. Be careful not to burn them.

Flatbreads should be eaten within two days, crackers can be stored in an airtight container for up to a week.

This is a wonderfully versatile alternative to regular cream that is delicious both hot and cold. I love it with my Wild berry, hazelnut and pecan galettes (page 213) or alongside my Chocolate and hazlenut skillet brownie cake (page 190).

# Cashew cream

**Makes about 240ml**

***For the sweet version***

*120g raw cashews, soaked for 3–5 hours but no longer*

*1 tsp vanilla extract*

*¼ tsp sea salt*

*2 tbsp maple syrup or honey (optional)*

***For the savoury version***

*120g raw cashews, soaked for 3–5 hours but no longer*

*½ tsp sea salt*

*1 tbsp harissa paste (optional)*

*1 tsp miso paste (optional)*

*1 tsp dried oregano (optional)*

*1 tsp lemon zest (optional)*

*1 tsp ground cumin (optional)*

Place the cashews along with 60–80ml water – use as much water as you like depending on how loose you want the cream to be – into a high speed blender. For a sweet cream add the vanilla, sea salt and maple syrup and for a savoury cream add the sea salt and two or three of the additional options, although I wouldn't recommend mixing harissa and miso. Blitz until creamy, scraping the sides at intervals. If you are using a food processor rather than a high-speed blender, you will need a little more patience, but persevere as a creamy result can be achieved.

This cream lasts for 3–4 days in the fridge in an airtight container.

When I first discovered infused butter I thought I had struck gold. I was in a restaurant in Switzerland and my fish arrived with a rather fancy meringue-shaped dome of what looked like pea purée but turned out to be basil-infused butter. The butter absolutely transformed the dish. Since then I have had a huge amount of fun with infused butters. I use them with fish, or melted into a bowl of otherwise slightly bland steamed vegetables. They are a wonderful way to transform humble bread and butter into delicious canapés, too. I love to serve thin slices of my Spelt, honey and walnut loaf (page 20) with a slather of Black olive and chive or my Sundried tomato and crispy rosemary butter.

For a cheat's way of cooling your butter quickly, place it in the freezer to firm up. You can also keep all the butters in the freezer for up to three months. A little trick is to allow the flavoured butters to firm up in the fridge, then cut them into circles and freeze the discs on a baking parchment-lined tray before transferring to resealable freezer bags so you have little pods of perfect butter to hand.

# Wickedly wonderful infused butters

**Each recipe makes 250g stick**

## Black olive and chive

*250g unsalted butter, softened*

*2 tbsp pitted, dry-cured olives, finely chopped*

*zest of 1 lemon*

*1 tbsp fresh lemon juice*

*2 tbsp finely chopped chives*

*sea salt and black pepper*

Either with a small whisk or fork, combine all the ingredients then transfer the butter to a piece of cling film or baking parchment and shape into a roll. Twist either end of the roll as though you were creating a giant sweet wrapper then place in the fridge until firm.

## Sundried tomato and crispy rosemary

*3 tbsp fresh rosemary leaves*

*roughly 6 sundried tomatoes, patted dry with paper towel if oily*

*250g unsalted butter, softened*

*1 tbsp lemon juice*

*sea salt and black pepper*

Preheat the oven to 160°C/325°F/gas mark 3. Begin by crisping the rosemary in the oven for about 10 minutes or until the needles are snappable.

Finely chop the crispy rosemary and the sundried tomatoes and transfer them to a small bowl with the softened butter.

Add the lemon juice, salt and pepper and either with a small whisk or fork vigorously combine all the ingredients. Transfer the butter to a piece of cling film or baking parchment and shape into a roll. Twist either end of the roll as though you were creating a giant sweet wrapper then place in the fridge until firm.

## Sesame and nori

*250g unsalted butter, softened*

*4–5 tbsp toasted sesame seeds, black or white*

*1 sheet of dried nori seaweed, crunched up into little pieces and finely chopped*

*½ tsp miso paste*

Either with a small whisk or fork combine all the ingredients then transfer the butter to a piece of cling film or baking parchment and shape into a roll. Twist either end of the roll as though you were creating a giant sweet wrapper then place in the fridge until firm.

# Toasted almond and ras el hanout

*250g unsalted butter, softened*

*1 small garlic clove, crushed or finely chopped*

*1 tbsp ras el hanout (or ½ tsp mixed spice, ½ tsp cayenne pepper, ½ tsp ground cumin, ½ tsp ground coriander seeds, ½ tsp ground ginger)*

*6 tbsp toasted flaked almonds (page 244), roughly chopped*

*pinch of salt*

If you are mixing your own spice blend, do this first. Do a taste test using your little finger to make sure it isn't too spicy – you are looking for more of a warming spice as opposed to off-the-charts-chilli-explosion.

Either with a small whisk or fork, combine all the ingredients then transfer the butter to a piece of cling film or baking parchment and shape into a roll. Twist either end of the roll as though you were creating a giant sweet wrapper then place in the fridge until firm.

Butter and coffee are two of life's greatest pleasures. I am a big fan of both and whisked together the two ingredients make something that is quite magical. This is one of my favourite things to make and bring as a gift to a dinner party. It is delicious spread on hot toast, melted onto Baked apples with cinnamon and toasted pecans (page 184) or slathered on thick slices of toasted Banana bread (page 22).

## Espresso

**Makes 250g**

*1 tsp or more light brown soft sugar or coconut sugar*

*1 tbsp strong-brewed coffee*

*250g unsalted butter, softened*

*1 tbsp fresh, finely ground coffee*

*1 tsp organic Dutch-processed cocoa powder (optional)*

*small pinch of salt (for more of a salted coffee butter, go with a bigger pinch)*

Combine the sugar and coffee liquid with just 1 tablespoon of the butter until it is well blended. Add the ground coffee, cocoa, if using, the remaining butter and the salt.

Either with a small whisk or fork combine all the ingredients then transfer the butter to a piece of cling film or baking parchment and shape into a roll. Twist either end of the roll as though you were creating a giant sweet wrapper then place in the fridge until firm.

These dips are perfect to serve with a few crudités when you are entertaining. They're also great when you're on the go and are often the key element to making my packed lunch box interesting.

# Three delicious dips

**Each serves 4–6**

## Black olive tapenade

*200g pitted, dry-cured or Niçoise black olives*

*1 large garlic clove, crushed or finely chopped*

*½ a small tin or 25g anchovies, drained and rinsed*

*2 tbsp capers, drained and rinsed*

*1 tbsp chopped thyme, tarragon or dried oregano*

*about 5 or more tbsp cold-pressed olive oil (add as needed)*

*1 tbsp fresh lemon juice, plus extra to taste*

*1 tbsp red wine vinegar*

If you are using a food processor, place the olives, garlic, anchovies, capers and herbs in the bowl and blend to a coarse purée. With the blade still spinning slowly, add the oil, lemon juice and vinegar. Taste and add more oil or lemon juice, if necessary.

If you are using a pestle and mortar, roughly chop the anchovies and capers, then add to the pestle and mortar with the garlic and herbs and pound until smooth. Repeat with the olives, leaving these a little rough in texture before gradually adding the olive oil, lemon juice and red wine vinegar. Taste and add more oil or lemon juice, if necessary.

Store in the fridge, covered, for 3–4 days.

## Artichokus *(creamy artichokes and tahini)*

*450g artichoke hearts (I usually use canned, drained)*

*3 tbsp tahini*

*zest and juice of 1 lemon*

*3 tbsp cold-pressed olive oil*
*sea salt and black pepper*

Combine the ingredients in a food processor, blend until smooth and season to taste.

## Tomatosolata *(creamy roasted cherry tomato)*

*300g cherry tomatoes*

*2 tbsp tahini*

*sea salt and black pepper*

Preheat the oven to 220°C/425°F/gas mark 7.

Roast the tomatoes on a lightly oiled roasting tray for about 20 minutes or until their skins have split and they are releasing some juice and sizzling.

Transfer the tomatoes to a bowl, add the tahini, salt and pepper and whisk vigorously with a fork until everything has incorporated to form a pale red dip.

These are delicious to serve as little nibbles when you are entertaining. You can be creative with the spice you choose. I like sumac but dried rosemary or a mix of cayenne pepper and mixed spice are delicious too. Be sure not to let your oven get too hot as the nuts will burn.

## Tahini and sumac-crusted walnuts

**One small bowl**

*100g walnuts*

*1½ tbsp tahini*

*2 tsp tamari or soy sauce*

*½ tsp ground sumac, or a pinch of cayenne pepper and mixed spice*

Preheat the oven to 120°C/225°F/gas mark ¼ and line a baking tray with parchment.

Combine all the ingredients in a small bowl and ensure that all the walnuts are well coated.

Transfer them to the baking tray and bake for 15–20 minutes or until they smell fragrant and the tahini has dried and crusted. Keep an eye on them and make sure they don't burn – don't worry if the tahini glaze seems a little wet in places as they will dry out as they cool.

You can keep these in an airtight container in the fridge for about a week, but I think they are best served just cooled.

These are a staple food in my kitchen and fantastic for jazzing up any meal. I tend to make them in large batches and keep them in old jam jars so that I always have them on hand to add to recipes. The method is quite simple, only ever requiring a frying pan or baking tray. You don't even have to use oil so there isn't any washing up – always a bonus. Allow the nuts and seeds to cool before storing and add them to salads, soups, vegetable dishes and dips.

# Toasted seeds and nuts

## Pan method

Place the nuts or seeds in a dry frying pan over a medium heat and toss until they begin to smell fragrant. You'll notice that pumpkin seeds and sesame seeds like to give a little pop! A few might even jump right out of the pan, so keep an eye on them.

### Almonds

The time will vary but as a general rule I would say it takes 10–12 minutes to toast whole almonds (although I prefer to use the oven method here – see opposite), 7–8 minutes to toast roughly chopped almonds, and 3–5 for flaked or sliced. Make sure you keep the temperature low when toasting flaked almonds and keep a close eye on them as they can burn quickly. I use almonds on everything from pancakes to salads.

### Cashews

Delicious on stir-fries, salads and soups but also on sweet things, too. Cashews have a wonderful natural sweetness that lends itself very well to tart fruit such as rhubarb. I usually toast them in the pan whole for about 8–10 minutes before roughly chopping.

### Sunflower seeds

Wonderfully nutty when roasted, these are delicious blended into dips, thrown into pastries or used as crumble toppings. These usually take 8–10 minutes in the pan.

### Pumpkin seeds

These are the real jumpers, so watch them. You'll know they're nearly ready when you start to hear snap, crackle and pop. Some of their skins may split, too. I usually keep mine on the hob for 6–8 minutes.

### Sesame seeds

Very often I am lazy and buy these ready toasted but the taste seems to be even richer when you do it at home and I rather like the variation in toastiness. These will cook quickly so keep the flame down low. I generally cook them for no more than 5 minutes and keep them moving in the pan constantly as they can burn quickly.

## Oven method

### Almonds

Preheat the oven to 170°C/325°F/gas mark 3 and place the nuts on a dry baking tray in the oven for 10–15 minutes, or until they begin to smell fragrant.

### Hazelnuts, pecans and walnuts

I find that these three nuts work best when toasted in the oven. They have a higher oil content than most and need to be watched carefully to ensure they don't burn.

Preheat the oven to 160°C/325°F/gas mark 3 and place the nuts on a dry baking tray in the oven for 8–10 minutes or until they begin to smell fragrant. Shake the tray occasionally and check after 6 minutes to ensure they are not burning.

# Sustainable directory

I always try to eat what is in season, and you'll have noticed that my recipes try to create as little waste as possible. Stocks, soups and leftovers are all big features in my day-to-day kitchen life and I hope this book has inspired you to try this approach in your own cooking.

Food waste on an industry level is still is a real problem but there are some fantastic charities, companies, restaurants and even apps that are helping to tackle the issue. Many even allow you the opportunity to donate any long-life food products that you no longer need to those that do. Here are some of those brilliant organsiations that are helping to make a difference.

**Fare share** – www.fareshare.org.uk

**Food cloud** – www.food.cloud

**FoodCycle** – www.foodcycle.org.uk

**Food Tank** – www.foodtank.com

**Love Food Hate Waste** – www.lovefoodhatewaste.com

**Plan ZHeroes** – www.planzheroes.org

**SILO restaurant Brighton** – http://www.silobrighton.com/

**The Felix Project** – www.thefelixproject.org

**The Sustainable Food Trust** – www.sustainablefoodtrust.org

**The Sustainable Restaurant Association** – www.thesra.org

**Too Good to Go App** – Find this on the app store and at www.toogoodtogo.co.uk

**Olio App** – Find this on the App store and at www.olioex.com

# Index

# Acknowledgements


There are so very many people to thank for helping me to write this book. I think people and experiences shape anything creative that I do, whether that's a painting, a story – or a lunch. Most, if not all of these recipes stem from moments and memories that were often shared with another. The tranquil moments in the early hours of the morning making phone calls to my Oma discussing what cakes we were going to make that week and what needed eating from the freezer; sharp, sour-sweet herrings chased with short black coffees in Amsterdam's Dam square with my Opa pa; and endless hours spent sitting cross-legged on the counter top whilst I watched my mother cook. Mumma you taught me how it's done and I owe any kitchen style and recipe secrets to learning from you. I also want to thank my father for always believing that I could do anything even when I didn't. Thank you for always being there when things got tough – and thank you for being my toughest food critic. Natasha and William thank you for being so patient whilst I rearranged, fussed and photographed the supper table and thank you for enduring all the pancake tests, sloppy cakes and bizarre food combinations over the years. I owe you both peanut butter cookies.

Freddie, thank you for being my rock, for making me laugh even when I burnt both breakfast and your jumper. Thank you for all the chopping, peeling and late-night, last-minute stops to the corner shop for ingredients, and thank you for keeping me company in the kitchen even when you were exhausted! You make me the happiest person. No one makes me laugh more than you and I cannot wait to cook together from this book. I promise lots of breakfasts in bed!

Thank you to my wonderful team at Orion; to Tamsin English and Amanda Harris for believing in me, to Abi Hartshorne for helping to design a beautiful book, to Andrew Burton for taking divine photos and Sophie Fox for keeping the shoot and everything else organized. Thanks to Mima Sinclair for being just godsmackingly brilliant (I hope I have half the golden energy you did when I am about to have a baby), and to Emily Barrett for being the most kind and patient editor one could hope for (there is no way I could have got through the final edits without you).

Thank you to my wonderful agent Cathryn Summerhayes – you always made me feel like I could do it, and I feel more determined to do everything having you at my side.

Thank you to all my wonderful friends; to Alex, Ben, Harriet, Sophie, Lily, Linda, Rhi, Monique and Zsa Zsa – you guys are the best. I cannot wait to all have supper soon.

And lastly, thank you to everyone who has bought this book. Ever since I can remember I have wanted to write a real cookbook, and as I write this now I am pinching myself that it is really real. Thank you for supporting me. I hope that some of the recipes and stories within this book give you some of the joy that writing them gave me – and, hopefully, stories and recipes of your own.

Born and bred in London, Alexandra has always been a firm believer in using seasonal, sustainable and quality ingredients. Her first company – Punch Foods – was founded on the principle that we should enjoy eating well without compromising on taste, and her Superseeds went on to be sold at Selfridges, Planet Organic and Ocado. As well as menu developing and food styling, Alexandra now hosts regular sustainable supper clubs and cookery classes at her home in North London.

First published in Great Britain in 2017 by Orion Publishing Group Ltd
Carmelite House, 50 Victoria Embankment, London, EC4Y 0DZ

An Hachette UK Company

10 9 8 7 6 5 4 3 2 1



A CIP catalogue record for this book is available from the British Library.

ISBN: 9781409169154

Photography: Andrew Burton
Design and art direction: Abi Hartshorne
Props: Tamzin Ferdinando
Food styling: Alexandra Dudley and Mima Sinclair

Printed and bound in Italy by Printer Trento S.r.l.

www.orionbooks.co.uk